Horse Welfare
a window on the equine world

Christopher Hall

Whittles Publishing

Published by
Whittles Publishing Ltd.,
Dunbeath,
Caithness, KW6 6EG,
Scotland, UK
www.whittlespublishing.com

© 2023 C. Hall
ISBN 978-184995-548-5

Previous hardback edition
Horse Welfare: Use Not Abuse
ISBN 978-184995-163-0, 2015

Printed by 4edge Limited, UK

'I can hear the creak of the saddle and the clop and clink of hoofs as we cross the bridge over the brook by Dundell Farm; there is a light burning in the farmhouse window, and the evening star glitters above a broken drift of half-luminous cloud. 'Only three miles more, old man', I say, slipping to the ground to walk alongside of him for a while.'

(*Memoirs of a Fox-Hunting Man*, Siegfried Sassoon)

The sadness is that a book like *'Horse Welfare, Use not Abuse'* should still need to be written after so many years of campaigning by charities such as World Horse Welfare. Indeed, matters seem to be getting worse as a result of over-breeding, doping and indiscriminate horse trading at markets where welfare is of little interest to those involved.

The greatest suffering continues to be in the inhumane transportation of horses across country borders to slaughter houses, matched only by the thousands of horses, donkeys and mules working long hours in the developing world. In these countries, the wellbeing of the horse may be just as significant as that of a child because, without a horse to fetch and carry, the very viability of family life can suffer. And yet it is still difficult for some to recognise the value of working animals in these situations.

While those struggling for survival may be forgiven for their failure to care adequately for their animals through ignorance or poverty, in equestrian ownership in more developed countries there is surely no excuse for inadequate care.

Christopher Hall brings an extensive knowledge and experience to this book which challenges all riders and owners to raise standards and refuse to accept the easy option, or worse, in their pursuit of success. His book is a valuable contribution to a campaign launched many years ago by Ada Cole and to which I have been pleased to lend my support.

Anne

Contents

Foreword

Equine welfare is an issue that should be paramount to all those who work with horses, donkeys and mules, from owners with one much-loved horse or pony to those working in elite equestrian sport, so this book remains as relevant as ever. The horse-human partnership in all its guises is at the centre of what World Horse Welfare strives to improve around the world and this authoritative first-hand account demonstrates clearly why our mission is vital. From the working equids who are so vital to the families who depend on them, to "low value" horses sold at markets by unscrupulous traders through to top-level sport and racehorses, this book shines an informative light on many corners of the equestrian world and will be a fascinating read for anyone with an interest in horses.

Roly Owers
Chief Executive, World Horse Welfare

Acknowledgements

I now have a chance to thank many people for their help and encouragement in the writing of this book.

My wife, Susanna, was advised by one of her flat mates before we became engaged, "Why not marry the man, look after him and be a mother to his horses?" What a result, and thank goodness she did because we have been able to do so many of the things referred to in this book together. I have been very fortunate.

While I was the Jockey Club Disciplinary Chairman I worked closely with Nigel McFarlane who was in charge of that department and knows the rules of racing so well. He has been invaluable in correcting a number of errors that I had made. Horse racing is a great sport but it is not immune from problems some of which I have taken the liberty of raising - I hope in a useful way.

Roly Owers has been highly effective since becoming Chief Executive of World Horse Welfare in 2008 and I must thank him and all his team, in particular the Field Officers, the Farm Managers in UK and the HQ staff who were always ready to help and advise. There is a great feeling of personal involvement both in the UK and across the world and I pay tribute to all those who carry out the charity's work, in particular in Central America, South Africa, Lesotho and Senegal. I am very proud to have been part of it and thank all those that I worked with for their support.

Bob Whittington has helped me collect my thoughts and kept "my nose to the grindstone" as I worked on the text, Without his advice, interest and involvement the book, much of which is based on the diaries that I kept at the time, would never have been written.

Finally, I must thank my publisher, Keith Whittles, for his interest, enthusiasm and tolerance waiting for the finished manuscript.

There are so many other people that I may not have named but who have influenced me about the essential goodness of those who care for their horses and donkeys and for that I will always be grateful.

Christopher Hall

Introduction

It is hard for me to think of a more satisfying pastime than riding my horse across beautiful countryside. For some, though, it seems hard to consider working with horses without breaking all laws of compassion and inflicting cruelty in a drive to make money.

My life had revolved around two things – the law and my love of horses – until, in my second 'career', the two became inextricably linked. Working with the leading charity World Horse Welfare, I applied what I had learned as a lawyer to my all-consuming passion for the protection and welfare of horses in the glamorous worlds of show jumping and racing, and then to the desperate plight of ordinary working horses at home and around the globe.

I would not have traded for anything my time with the Jockey Club, which was in complete control of racing when I became a member in 1990. There were daily challenges, complaints, furious rows and accusations from all quarters: if we weren't incompetent amateurs, we were defending the indefensible – cruelty to the very animals we claimed to cherish. We interfered too much in the use of whips, or didn't interfere enough. We were portrayed as cowards in the face of criticism from professionals with vested interests. One thing, though, is certain: for better or for ill, depending on one's point of view, we were, at least, in control. As different nations become more dominant and different types of racing become more attractive to the public, what organisation, if any, has that same grip on British racing affairs today?

While the jockeys, trainers, show jumpers and eventers I have encountered have a great love of horses, there are always exceptions who hit the headlines, breaking the rules, even resorting to drug abuse to gain that extra yard, and who are prepared to offend repeatedly, dragging the sport's reputation down with them. The only way to beat the drug abusers is to make the penalties so severe that it is not worth taking the risk; plans to increase suspensions and to prevent those convicted and their horses from ever associating with professional competitors, even banning offenders from teaching or producing competition horses, must surely be welcomed. But make no mistake: we are playing a catch-up game as the drugs masking the abuse become ever more sophisticated and the rewards for the wrongdoers vastly outstrip the funds available to combat the crime. Despite the fact that the odds are heavily stacked against those policing equestrian events, we must, for the sake of the horses and the sport, keep trying. Equestrianism is not alone in this fight, as drug abuse in other sports such as athletics appears to be rampant; it is a collective battle which we must all join.

Away from the glamour of racing, working horses around the world, toiling day in, day out, deserve our protection from neglect and ignorance. Horses can't complain. They put up with the abuse until they can take no more and, silently, give up the will to continue. When we have done with them, we turn a blind eye in their final days as unscrupulous traders transport them hundreds of miles across borders, crammed into lorries for days without adequate water or food, to be slaughtered to satisfy human palates. It must stop and we must speak up for them in their suffering.

If nothing else, I hope this book will alert those with just a passing interest in horses, such as the individual who only once a year places a bet on the Grand National or the Derby, to look out for these lesser creatures. For others, I hope there will be some insight into the professional equestrian world, what has happened in the past and what continues today from the point of view of the regulators, the men and women who usually operate unseen and who are regularly chastised for their decisions. Many of the jockeys and trainers who have been punished by a disciplinary hearing will surely disagree, but our intention, as stewards, is always to apply common sense in our judgements and in our interpretation of the rules and regulations.

There is also a warning to the professionals in the world of equestrian sport that they have a duty of care not just to the horses, but to the sport they enjoy. They must drive out the miscreants and refuse to turn a blind eye to abuse, however mild, even if a big name is involved, because a failure to do so will result in lower attendances and ultimately, even, the demise of the sport. The public have many alternatives vying for their attention. If they spot malpractice, often via a TV action replay, they will first protest and then walk away, and with them will go not just the livelihoods of jockeys and trainers, but of the countless numbers of farriers, grooms, feed suppliers and manufacturers.

It strikes me that, while the years may have passed, the same questions persist. Do dedicated amateurs have a valid opinion or should we only have professional stewards at race meetings? Should jockeys be allowed to whip? If they should, how much? Should French racehorses be allowed to jump hurdles as two-year-olds? Issues such as doping may seem new but are simply cheating in another form, and cheating will always be with us. There are challenges even to the morality of racing horses as two-year-olds, before they are fully developed, and perennial concerns about the dangers of steeplechasing.

In large part this is a story about one charity among many. Lobbying hard for the fair treatment of sports horses, it is always fighting to help horse and donkey owners in developing countries learn new ways to look after the animals on which they depend and, by teaching them, aiming to spread the word about the importance of animal welfare. Any improvement in the health of a horse can translate immediately into economic benefit for the owner's family, then a village and ultimately a whole community. This is a single, integrated process. A tourist pony-trekking in Haiti or Lesotho is helping the local economy, but unless the pony is fit, its owner's job will be short-lived, his family will go hungry and poverty will be perpetuated.

The vast majority of working horses and donkeys suffering in the developing world are doing so not because their owners are cruel, but because they do not, in general, have the wherewithal to improve the lot of the animals upon which they and their families depend. If shoes and harness don't fit, it is because the owners have to make do with any material they can find – scrap metal, wire, wood and old blankets – to fashion something that passes for tack. These creatures are not a luxury but an absolute necessity; they carry and pull heavy loads, help bring in the crops and usually provide the only form of transport.

When aid is sent to a disaster zone, the first step in delivering support very often depends upon horses and donkeys, and yet they are seldom, if ever, mentioned. If a vet is needed, yet the nearest one is many tens of kilometres away, the only treatment a horse is likely to receive will be rudimentary and sometimes brutal. This book has been written, above all, in praise of an animal which has served us well and which will continue to serve us, work for us and entertain us, as it always has done.

Christopher Hall

1 | BEGINNINGS

Just before Christmas 2013, I received an email from colleagues at the South African Cart Horse Protection Association, saying that they had managed to rehome five badly-neglected horses at their farm just outside Cape Town. I was delighted, but sadly could top their achievement. Our World Horse Welfare charity had just picked up 63 derelict horses and ponies and had taken them to one of our farms, in Norfolk. It was a terrible indictment of these creatures' treatment in an animal-loving country, but I have witnessed such neglect throughout my life and fear it is getting worse. It is not peculiar to the British, of course: people the world over seem to think horses exist to be used and abused.

I started working with World Horse Welfare (WHW) in 2005. We have four farms dotted throughout the UK, near Aberdeen, Blackpool and in Somerset as well as in Norfolk, and they have never been busier. They are all working to capacity and the worst situation is found in the affluent south of England, where the field officers get calls about potential neglect every day of the year.

My direct involvement with WHW came after what you might call a deep immersion course in working with horses in one capacity or another since I was a boy. Although a lawyer by training, I am a horseman by inclination, and I have been lucky enough to work with some of the best equestrian men and women on the international circuit. Even at the highest level, though, I have found that the horses we admire so much can be mistreated to gain an extra advantage. A desire to win is not the only reason: cruelty can be caused by ignorance, economic circumstance or even fashion. All three of these are having an impact today but it is clear to me that profit is the principal enemy.

It was as a member of the Pony Club, that great mainstay of riding education, that I was first alerted to what people thought looked good for animals, when in fact it is merely a human vanity. At the time, I happened to have a cob called Mr Briggs whose tail had been docked. This amputation of the tail is to stop the 'skirt', or long hairs, growing out. It was typically carried out when horses pulled ploughs and carts, to stop their tails getting caught up in the mechanism, and presumably saved time having to plait every morning. Today it is banned in many parts of the world, including Great Britain, Norway, parts of Australia and some parts of the US. As a boy I was blissfully unaware of this, the docking having been performed by a previous owner, but it was enough to draw comment from a local RSPCA member at a Pony Club camp at Plumpton racecourse, where I was competing. This Mrs Hayes Newington gave me the message loud and clear: horses are living creatures, not ornaments, and their tails have many purposes, including swishing flies away, indicating alarm or protecting the horse in bad weather. She suggested a replica raffia tail, which might have been impractical, but I have never forgotten the reprimand.

A little later in life I was taught another short, sharp lesson about putting the welfare of my horse before my own needs. I was 18 and doing my national service as Second Lieutenant Hall with the 5th Royal Inniskilling Dragoon Guards, 'the Skins', at Catterick. Like many other members of cavalry regiments, we were allowed to keep our horses in stables at the barracks and encouraged to go hunting to improve our riding. On one occasion we had been out with the Bedale Hunt and on our return I handed my horse over to Sergeant Power in the regimental stables, had a bath, read the newspapers and, in due course, found myself in a small anteroom having a drink, waiting to go in for dinner. The senior major in the mess, Peter Martel - I later became his solicitor - was standing in front of the fire, hands behind his back. With him was Richard Keightley, the senior subaltern and a regular soldier, who asked if I had been down to the stables to check on my horse. I replied that I had not. He retorted that he had been to see his and that I should check mine. I said I would go straight after dinner, but he ordered me to go immediately. It was a very good lesson: my horse had looked after me all day and, while I knew that he had been fed and watered, the least I could do was make sure he was settled and had not suffered any injury. I still check my horses in the field every day and those in the stables last thing at night.

Today, with no Sergeant Power to take my horse after a long day's hunting, I get back to the horsebox, wash the horse down, give him water and hay and make sure he is comfortable. By the time I have done that the other followers have eaten all the tea. Keightley went on to become a Major General and Commandant at Sandhurst Military Academy, no doubt instructing his cadets about the importance of caring for their equipment as well as doing their rigorous training. 'Look after your horse, look after your rifle,' would be the message 'and they will look after you.'

For some truly passionate riders, the horse will always come first, even over nearest and dearest. My commanding officer was called Cecil 'Monkey' Blacker, and we were all in awe of him. He was awarded the Military Cross for his bravery during the Normandy Landings in June 1944, rose to be a general and was knighted.

He was a fanatical horseman, international show jumper and pentathlete. On one occasion, so legend has it, he was out hunting, leading the field as usual, when his wife 'Zulu' had a crashing fall. Blacker is said to have turned and shouted to the nearest subaltern, 'Take care of Zulu!' before galloping away. Nothing would be allowed to spoil either his or his horse's day out.

After my two-year spell of National Service, I left the army in 1956 to go up to Cambridge University to read law. This is where my enthusiasm for working with animals really began. It was also my first introduction to competition: little did I know how the law and the professional riding scene would eventually be combined in my life. I discovered that, if I was prepared to be whipper-in for the university drag hounds, my horse would be kept for nothing, and before long, while still an undergraduate, I had my first ride in a point-to-point. I had taken a step into the professional equestrian world where they played for high stakes at the very top of the game, and in time I would be having a say in whether or not the rules were being broken.

In the meantime, I had also taken a keen interest in the highly charged and super-competitive world of show jumping, in which a similar informality still applied when it came to handing out jobs. I had written to the show director, Colonel Mike Ansell, the renowned blind show director who was later knighted, asking if I might become a steward at the Royal International Horse Show (RIHS), which in those days was held at the White City stadium. It had been built for the 1908 Summer Olympics and in its day hosted a variety of events, from athletics, greyhound racing and speedway to a match in the 1966 Football World Cup and the RIHS, before being demolished in 1985. I am convinced that my selection as a steward was due entirely to my short career in the 'Skins', as Colonel Ansell was a former colonel in my old regiment.

I was just 21 years old when I began, surrounded by some of the great names in international show jumping, although initially I found myself watching over the outside collecting ring rather than being permitted into the main arena. Apart from helping shepherd the competitors in and out of the arena, there was also a duty to keep an eye on the riders and how they were treating their horses. I never had cause to reprimand anyone, but perhaps the very presence of a steward had the desired effect.

My appointment at the RIHS also gave me an *entrée* as a steward at the Horse of the Year Show at Wembley in 1959. On one occasion, I was on duty in the collecting ring when I bumped into an old friend from my Cambridge days, Anneli Drummond-Hay. She was by then a highly successful rider and had won Badminton on her horse of a lifetime, Merely-a-Monarch. She said she had had a bad morning. She had a horse called Bushranger by White Way, the leading point-to-point sire of the day, but he had broken down and, as she could not afford to keep him, would have to be put down. I asked what he looked like and - slightly unusually, given the occasion - she produced a photo out of her pocket. He seemed more like a middle-weight hunter and I liked the look of him. I had neither the opportunity nor the money to race him at the time, so I thought I would get him home and put him away for a year to recover. I told Anneli that I had just received my annual stipend of £100 from Her Majesty's Government for being on the army emergency reserve list, and she accepted this as payment. I was still an articled clerk earning just £3 a week in London, but living at home in Sussex with my parents. I kept the deal quiet from them and had Bushranger delivered secretly to a friendly farmer nearby. Eventually, of course, they found out, and my father called it 'gross extravagance'. He was right!

The point I would make about Bushranger, in the context of this book about horse welfare, is that he had been 'fired' to help his tendons recover. Thermocautery or firing, as it is more commonly known, was first written about in AD 500 and remains to this day a source of fierce debate among vets in the equestrian world. Under sedation, the horse has a red-hot firing iron placed against the lower leg to try and heal the torn tendons. The procedure was banned for a time in the UK. Is it animal welfare or animal cruelty? The debate will continue, but Bushranger proved to be by far the best horse I rode in point-to-points, winning many races, helped along with the occasional dose of phenylbutazone, or 'bute', prescribed by the distinguished vet, Peter Scott-Dunn. I have since had another horse which has also been 'fired'.

Peter was not only responsible for introducing phenylbutazone, an anti-inflammatory drug, to the equine world but was also vet to Britain's Olympic equestrian team and looked after the Queen's horses. Today the use of bute in racehorses differs around the world. Some states in America allow horses on bute to race because, the argument goes, it does not enhance performance but merely brings the horse back to the level of performance it would have were it not in pain. What's more, they say, without its use they might not have enough sound horses to race.

In the UK, horses on this drug - or any other - may not race. In America, the drug furosemide, commonly known as Lasix, is regularly and legally used. It is a diuretic which makes a horse lose some 2% of its body weight and is said – although opinions differ – to reduce bleeding in the horse's lungs when it runs. Its critics say that this not only provides a performance advantage, but that Lasix can conceal the presence of other, prohibited drugs. It is ridiculous that the restriction on the use of the drug varies from state to state. Naturally, I think horses should be run Lasix-free. Nobody knows the long term effect of this drug – some suggest that it might reduce calcium levels, leading to weaker bones. Happily, in 2014, the first signs began to appear that Lasix could be banned once and for all in US racing, as leading British trainers, like Jamie Osborne, the trainer of Toast of New York, who has won in the States and was second in the American Breeders' Cup World Championships in October 2014, and John Gosden, British flat racing champion trainer in 2012, stated quite bluntly that it was a performance-enhancing drug. I accept that it is impossible immediately to rule out all horses that have been given Lasix in the past, but it could be done over a three or four year span. A complete ban is what's needed long-term, although not all US trainers are in favour of that, despite the potential positive impact for the sport. Ogden 'Dinny' Phipps, former chairman of the Jockey Club in the US, warned during a speech at the IFHA Paris Arc Conference: 'Research has confirmed our medication policies in North America are alienating current fans, prospective fans and prospective sponsors, not to mention animal rights activists, media and congressional leaders.'

Bute worked for me, though, and for many horse owners it may mean the difference between enabling a horse to live a long and pain-free life or putting it down; for many years I was able to ride Bushranger out every morning before leaving for work in London.

This brings me to the duty we have to our horses. Keeping a horse brings chores as well as pleasures, and owners have obligations: horses have to be exercised in fair weather or foul, and that means riding them regularly, even if one has to get up early to do so before work. Horses cannot be left to stew in a stable all day, nor can they be turned out in the field for too long. If nothing else, their hooves need checking because – and this is clearly a surprise to some – their feet continue to grow; their hooves really need trimming every six weeks to keep them healthy. Roly Owers, who took over from the retiring Chief Executive John Smales in 2007, tells a good story about a mother who said she had just bought a pony for her daughter. Roly congratulated her but was stunned by her reply. Yes, she said, it was marvellous, particularly as the pony had come with shoes on so she would never have to bother about that again.

And it's not just their feet that grow. A young girl in Scotland acquired a pony called Digger. She thought he was a sweet little foal which would suit her well, competing in local gymkhanas and hacking out near her stables. But Digger grew and grew and grew. By the time he reached 16 hands he was already too much for his owner and WHW agreed to take him into our farm in Scotland. But Digger wasn't done. He just kept growing and was soon heading towards the Guinness Book of Records level. He was too big to be moved by ordinary horsebox or trailer. Someone then had the brilliant idea of offering him to the Household Cavalry for training as a drum horse. An inspector was sent up to assess his potential and they agreed that they would take Digger on for trial as a 'recruit'. They kept him for over two years before they decided he just wasn't sound enough to do the job, so we now have him back again on the farm outside Aberdeen. He is about 19 hands.

A key point to note here is that WHW took Digger back, as we are prepared to do for any horse we let go. They are never sold, only sent out on loan or, as we prefer, rehomed. We will always take them back to one of our farms to make sure they haven't learned any bad habits because we will want to offer them as a hack or suitable child's pony and have to be careful of the WHW reputation, but we would, of course, prefer that they settled for good at their new home. The horses have to be well schooled as well as in good health; we are saving horses and preparing them for a working life at the same time as tackling cruelty head-on.

These two anecdotes point to ignorance, an aspect of horse welfare which I will address in more detail later. People, usually well-meaning parents, very often buy a pony for their child without realising what they are taking on. It is not the same as looking after a cat, which will spend most of its day asleep or grooming itself, often working at night. Ponies and horses are, at minimum, a twice-daily commitment, with numerous chores in between.

My immersion course in horses was indeed all-consuming and was later to include racing. My family lived in Eridge, East Sussex and I knew that John, Marquess of Abergavenny, a keen race-goer and owner, and previous Master of the Eridge Fox Hounds, had been involved as an owner and was a leading member of the Jockey Club. He subsequently became the Queen's representative at Ascot. Following a meeting with him to plead the cause of a tenant who had fallen behind with his rent, I rather diffidently approached him, plucking up the courage to say that I would like to be a racecourse steward locally in the future, if a vacancy occurred. I boldly considered myself somehow qualified as I had competed in several point-to-point races and had had my first winner in 1961 in the Members' Race at the Eridge Hunt meeting at Kippings Cross, Tunbridge Wells, a true cross-country course through the hop gardens. He put in a good word for me and, in due course, on 21 August 1966, I got a letter from Commander Egerton, a somewhat daunting character who lived in nearby Robertsbridge. He wrote saying that, much to his regret, a new rule had been introduced forcing stewards to retire at the age of 75, which meant that he had to stand down. He said that he had been assured by Lord Abergavenny that I was the man to take over. It was as simple and informal as that, and so I was appointed a steward with just a few point-to-point winners and a Pony Club 'B' Test to my name.

It is precisely this informal, almost casual approach that I would like to emphasise. It was a relatively serious position: money was changing hands at the bookmakers, after all, and jockeys and trainers are financially affected if results are altered. The decision to appoint me was perhaps based on the knowledge that they were appointing someone whose main interest was in horses, which some might argue is strangely lacking today in the amateur equestrian world. People believe they have a right to own a horse or pony regardless of their level of knowledge of – or indeed sympathy for – these uncomplaining creatures. No one, quite simply, should have that right – prospective owners should have to demonstrate that they are capable of caring for a horse. My work with WHW has shown me all too clearly that many people are not equipped to look after horses, and there may soon be a case for imposing the same sort of licensing system that we had for dogs before it was abolished in 1987.

There are probably more than one million horses and ponies in the UK, with 250,000 people working full- or part-time with them in some capacity. It all needs monitoring. I have no doubt that most people set out with the best intentions: they just want to go out for a hack and then try a few local shows. But the interest then wears off, the early morning starts to feed the horses and the caring for them during the wet winter months begin to seem less appealing or perhaps the horse just gets old. People will say: I've still got my old horse, he's 26. When asked what they do with him they say: Oh, he's out in the field. In other words, he is ignored and abandoned. Quite honestly he would be better off with a bullet in the head, just as I would be if ignored and abandoned. After your horse has looked after you, as I learned at Catterick, it is your turn to give something back while he is healthy, if a little decrepit. Don't believe for one moment that this is a rare occurrence; I regret that neglect, sometimes through ignorance or circumstance, is all too common the world over, as the evidence gleaned by WHW demonstrates.

In short, I was now set on a path which I happily allowed to tear me between a career in the law and a passion for horses. Even while serving my five-year apprenticeship at 11 Old Jewry, London as an articled clerk with a leading firm, Clifford Turner, as it was then called, my eye would wander. I would get bored with the London grind and on occasion would go and watch the racing with the lift man. Once during Royal Ascot, I swept into his flat on the top floor and found the senior partner, Raymond Clifford Turner, already seated in front of the television. We discussed the racing but he had no idea I worked for him. The senior partner was far too busy to bother with trainees, but then he always did walk round the office with his head down. Years later, when I was stewarding at Plumpton where he had a runner, I went and up and introduced myself. He was none the wiser. What an impression I must have made.

There is a dichotomy in the British psyche. We profess to adore these wonderful creatures and everyone, from the Pony Club to the older surviving members of the cavalry regiments, has countless anecdotes of their admiration for, and devotion to, their horses. And yet, while dogs and cats probably outnumber horses and ponies ten to one in the UK alone, there are possibly ten times more charities for horses than there are for our other favourite pets.

It may have all started with *Black Beauty*, Anna Sewell's wonderful novel written back in 1877. Bringing us right up to date, we have *War Horse*, Michael Morpurgo's 1982 novel, which was belatedly discovered, became a runaway success on the London stage and then turned into a Steven Spielberg blockbuster. Before *War Horse*, though, we might never have received a call about the 69 horses which had to be rescued by WHW. People would not even have bothered to report it or even ask themselves what all those horses were doing, standing around with nothing to eat or drink.

Tragically, 2014 opened with another disaster: torrential rain and the worst floods for 250 years in the south of England. Houses in Somerset, along the south-west coastline and the upper reaches of the Thames Valley were swamped as rivers burst their banks, and animals suffered too, as fields turned into lakes.

The British Horse Society, which itself responded to more than 8,000 welfare cases in 2013, was one of the many charities involved in the aftermath. The *Horncastle News* quoted its Director of Equine Policy, Lee Hackett: 'Horses drowning in flooded fields, starving to death, riddled with worms and lice, poor or non-existent hoof care or dumped to fend for themselves may sound like something from a hundred years ago in the fields of the Somme, but sadly it is Britain in 2014. The horse has been a loyal servant to mankind and is an integral part of our heritage. We owe him so much yet, now when he needs us, we are spectacularly failing him.'

WHW, together with the RSPCA, HorseWorld and Redwings, released a report in June 2013 warning that 'over 7,000 horses in England and Wales are at risk of suffering.' Complaints being investigated by the RSPCA alone have risen 16 fold since 2012, and Redwings said calls to their emergency line were up by 75 per cent in the first quarter of 2013. Is this a sign that people are becoming more aware that there are charities which will react to a call?

As the Keightleys and the Blackers taught me during my national service, one learns by example, and it is probably the glamour of the professional circuit, the racing, the show jumping and the Olympics which attract people - youngsters and, worse still, adults with an eye for a fast buck – to horses. It is incumbent on the professional riders to set the highest standards, not only in the way they look after their horses away from the spotlight, but also in the way they perform in public and, increasingly, in front of the TV cameras. The way they ride, whether they beat their horses when they refuse a jump, jag them viciously in the mouth to bring them under control when they run out, or kick too hard; all these things are noted and copied by young riders who come to believe that this is acceptable behaviour. It is not.

2 | THE PROFESSIONAL CIRCUIT

In the late 1950s, the method used to train horses to reach their peak was, by today's standards, fairly rudimentary; some might call it rough and verging on cruel. If riders had a horse which they thought had show jumping potential but felt that it should be trying harder, it was not uncommon to put wire on the poles to make the horse pick its feet up. The technique of raising a pole as the horse jumped was known as 'rapping'. Today, techniques have moved on: some riders have been known to 'wrap' their horses' hind legs in weighted boots to encourage them to flick their feet away from the jump.

At top-level competitions such as the Horse of the Year Show, which used to be broadcast after the nine o'clock news every night on BBC TV, the stewards help to police what goes on outside the arena and there is a steward in a bowler hat to make sure the riders are not abusing their horses. Most riders were exemplary. One of the great show jumpers of the 1950s and early 1960s was Raimondo d'Inzeo who, along with his brother Piero, cut quite a dash in their Italian army uniforms. General Raimondo, as he eventually became, was a gold medallist for Italy in the Rome Olympics in 1960 and he and his brother went on to become the first siblings to win gold and silver in an individual Olympic event which they contested together. They competed at the Royal International Horse Show every year. They were steeped in riding, their father, Carlo d'Inzeo, being chief instructor in the Royal Piedmontese Dragoons. It was notable that when Raimondo died, late in 2013, the heading on his obituary in the *Daily Telegraph* (25 January 2014) read: 'Olympic show jumping champion whose gentle handling of his horses set new standards for the sport.' The text went on: 'Above all, however, d'Inzeo was a superlative horseman who influenced future generations of riders in the way that he sought not to 'dominate' his horse but to achieve absolute harmony between horse and rider.'

This epitaph should be read by all budding riders. If those standards and approach were good enough for an Olympic gold medallist, then surely they are good enough for the rest of us. I have been lucky enough to work at many British international shows, but what goes on outside the arena in the privacy of someone's home is anyone's guess. I have been told that some well-known figures had places where they would 'sort out' their horses and I have no doubt that the phrase 'sorting out' says it all. On the other hand, the great stars do achieve tremendous results and they can't manage that unless the horse is trying. The only question is: are they trying because they are scared or because they enjoy it? I think one can safely say that Raimondo d'Inzeo never resorted to 'sorting out' his horses.

We do not have the manpower to police these matters away from the showgrounds. Unless a neighbour happens to see a horse being beaten up in a field and decides to approach the RSPCA, then we are unlikely ever to hear about it. The RSPCA inspector will appear and may turn out to know very little about horses, being more used to dealing with smaller animals, and so will call one of our WHW field officers to help. The owner will challenge the field officer: 'Can you see where this horse has been beaten up?' It can be an intimidating business, with animal inspectors facing thuggery and even the use of guns, being armed themselves with nothing more than a desire to help an animal. It takes courage and sometimes, as we shall see, a little subterfuge to gather evidence which will stand up in court.

The rule in racing today is that if a jockey marks a horse, then they have obviously hit it too hard, although some horses mark easily. In practice, it is a difficult thing to prove. What's needed is an official who is moderately qualified and prepared to stand up to a rider who may have years of international experience as a professional jockey and who regards stewards as amateurs with no practical knowledge.

Much has changed since the days of relying on a man in a bowler hat. Nowadays, there have to be vets on duty at all shows, which was unheard of 20 years ago. It makes sense, but it does add to the expense, which makes life difficult for some of the smaller events. People will therefore cut corners. At a village show it may only be necessary to have a vet on call. At a top show like Hickstead in West Sussex, the home of the Show Jumping Derby, vets would probably be seated with the judges, with the authority to ask a rider to trot a horse up if they thought it looked lame. This is seen in racing where the jockey is uncertain about the soundness of his horse at the start of a race: a vet may make the horse trot up and down before letting it run. The final decision is in the hands of the starter and the vet.

By contrast, at the amateur level, people still expect to be able to drag their horses in from the field with little preparation and enter them for competition. There is certainly no 'trot up' as there is before and after the cross-country day at the likes of Badminton and Burghley Horse Trials, where, much to the rider's dismay, it is not uncommon for a horse to be sent home as unsound. The 'trot up' is a very tense moment for everyone concerned. At local shows, there are still experienced judges who might refuse to judge a horse if they feel it is unsound, but that is as formal as it gets. This comes down, again, to ignorance rather than neglect on the part of owners and riders, but one is no less cruel than the other.

Science, or rather its misuse, has now come into the picture at the highest level. It used to be rare that anyone was found to be doping their horse or even to be wrongly accused of doing so. But the rules are strict and it is the rider's responsibility to know exactly what nutrition or veterinary medicine their horse is receiving. No one is immune and failed tests have cost Olympic medals.

In 2005, the German show jumping team lost its gold medal in Athens when Ludger Beerbaum's horse, Goldfever, failed a doping test. The judges found that the banned steroid betamethasone was contained in an ointment used to treat a skin irritation on the horse. The Judicial Committee accepted that Beerbaum had not deliberately tried to enhance the horse's performance. 'Nevertheless, the (rider) has failed to ensure that Goldfever has no prohibited substances in its systems during an international event,' ruled the FEI (International Federation for Equestrian Sports), the governing body of equestrian sports based in Lausanne, Switzerland, and the horse was disqualified.

The maintenance of top level, even amateur rides, has become so much more complicated than in the days when a basic feed and a hay net would suffice. The FEI, which is a signatory to the World Anti-Doping Agency (WADA) Code, has a policy precisely to protect the welfare of the horses from physical abuse or doping and, while it is up to vets to know what is and what is not allowed by referring to the FEI's approved 'medicine box', it is always the rider's responsibility to know what their horse is receiving.

More recently, in October 2013, the eventing world was stunned when the New Zealander, Jock Paget, an Olympic 2012 bronze medallist with the national eventing team, won the Burghley Horse Trials, was suspended then disqualified by the FEI. His horse, Clifton Promise, on which he had also won the Badminton Horse Trials the previous May, had tested positive for the banned sedative, reserpine. Another horse ridden by his mentor, Kevin McNab, also tested positive for the same substance. The two horses had been in adjacent temporary boxes at Burghley. Paget, who had just burst onto the eventing scene, becoming only the second rider to win Badminton on his debut, was temporarily suspended pending further testing and faced a two-year ban from competitions. As it was, the FEI stripped Paget of his victory at Burghley in a partial ruling, promoting fellow New Zealander, Andrew Nicholson, riding Avebury, to first place. (Andrew Nicholson and Avebury went on to win Burghley in 2014 as well making eventing history by becoming the first rider to win a four-star event in three consecutive years on the same horse). In addition to clarifying who had and who had not qualified to compete at Badminton the following year (May 2014), it was sending out a clear signal about hardening attitudes towards drug abuse.

It was all a tragic outcome for Paget who is obviously a talented star of the future and who, remarkably, had only begun riding at 18, having served an apprenticeship as a bricklayer. It took him less than two years to progress from never having jumped a fence to competing in a three-star eventing competition. The FEI eventually ruled that Paget and McNab should both be exonerated of any blame, after a herbal supplements supplier admitted responsibility for supplying the contaminated products. In a world of high standards and strict quality control, Roger Hatch of Sussex admitted mixing the supplement on his kitchen table with, according to the *Daily Telegraph*, 'a wooden spoon and plastic bowl.'

The penalties these days are, quite rightly, too severe to take a chance, although, to increase their chances of winning, all the top riders have a string of horses, possibly up to twenty, many of which are sponsored by individual owners, which makes it difficult for riders always to monitor every feed and every treatment because they travel so much. By contrast, the famous show jumper, Pat Smythe, when competing for Britain in the 1950s, had only two top horses: Prince Hal, an ex-racehorse, and, later, Tosca, on which she won many medals and regularly competed abroad.

In the days when top riders had relatively few horses, those horses had to be looked after. One could not take risks with them because, even at the top level, one might only have a couple of potential medal winners. On the other hand, and for the same reason, they probably did more work day to day. The average rider would certainly not have a yard full of horses, and not everyone had a trailer, let alone a horsebox, to take them back and forth to meets or shows. I remember clearly, in my younger days, hacking ten miles back home along the road, quite late, after a day's hunting; it was safer on the roads then, with less traffic. To that extent I have a feeling that horses then were tougher, more like everyday working horses, more utilitarian than the over-cosseted mounts of today. In racing, certainly, horses have become faster and more finely bred. The legs of some of the thoroughbreds are so slender, one wonders how they stand serious training. My wife, Susanna, and I used to do an hour and a half trotting on the road to toughen up my horses for point-to-points, and we did not, by and large, have lame horses. Maybe there is a lesson there.

I have always thought that point-to-point horses should be hunted properly, but I accept that there has to be a balance. What is the object of the exercise? Is it to go hunting, racing, show jumping or eventing? My old horse, now 22, who was hardly a speed machine, hunted and raced, and even won on occasion, with scarcely an off day. Our blacksmith might comment that the horse is 'pretty stiff behind – maybe a little bute would help?' and for my part, I give myself Ibuprofen when I am rather stiff after a long day. The rider, too, needs care.

There are many more competitions for people to enter these days, the Pony Club branches staging regular competitions for their members and visitors. My only caveat here is that horses need rest as well as exercise, and some parents, or their children, are perhaps too eager to enter every show, even many classes in a single show, as they chase the winner's rosette.

At the senior level, people don't think twice about travelling long distances in ever more luxurious lorries to compete in shows. While I paid £100 for Bush Ranger, essentially for amateur point-to-point race riding, people today happily pay £2,000 or £3,000 and still have no intention of doing very much more than hacking and occasionally entering a local show. Once there, they may be more concerned about getting kicked by another horse or finding themselves in an ill-prepared and rain-soaked arena.

On the subject of prices, the 2008 recession had a marked impact, certainly on horses and ponies at the lower end of the scale. My colleagues in WHW reported a worrying trend. One of our field officers summed it up: 'Anyone in the UK can go out and buy a horse. They are cheaper than they have ever been before. At the New Forest sales, it is possible to buy a pony for £5. We have been called to a tower block where a horse was being kept in a coal shed, the owners apparently thinking that would do. People seem to say: 'Oh I'll have a couple, put a bit of work in and sell them for a profit,' but they aren't selling. Colts have to be castrated, which costs £150 minimum, sometimes more; the costs of gelding are potentially very expensive. So people either ditch the colts or keep them entire, which has a knock-on effect because there are now more animals capable of breeding, and possibly ones which shouldn't be breeding because of their poor conformation. All these excess horses, which the charity is having to mop up, are often poor quality horses not capable of doing a job, which an animal of value would be, and in the end they may have to be put down.'

Sadly, this is an all-too-common experience and, because horses can be as cheap to buy as a bottle of wine, people seem to treat them in the same casual manner. Even the best intentions can lead to problems. WHW regularly has to visit dilapidated farms where someone has taken in more horses than they can handle. It usually begins on a small scale where the owners themselves 'rescue' a horse they felt was being neglected. In time, they become known as a rescue centre for horses, usually unofficial and unregistered, and before long find themselves overwhelmed and the very people accused of neglect. The UK has many unofficial animal sanctuaries, which have sprung up with little or no regulatory supervision.

There are no longer any veterinary checks at ports for competition or any other horses travelling between the UK, Ireland and mainland Europe. Competition horses, of course, travel in great comfort – a tired or stressed animal is not likely to perform well – but the newspapers still carry stories about the export of live animals destined for the slaughterhouse. While horsemeat is not harmful to humans, it remains a controversial subject in the UK, illustrated in 2013 by the discovery of horse DNA in processed meat being sold in some supermarkets.

WHW carried out its own investigation in 2013 at the port of Dover and on the French-Belgian border. It estimated that thousands of horses and ponies were possibly being exported under the pretence that they were for leisure or sport, but without any welfare or documentary checks.

Over one 48-hour weekend, there were 51 export shipments and 41 imports, in lorries capable of carrying between 2 and 22 horses, without any checks being carried out. WHW's CEO, Roly Owers, said: 'We have discovered this really murky trade in low financial value equines across Europe. It is not only a matter of equine welfare, it is also a huge problem for equine health and, as we have seen because of the relationship with the food trade and the food industry, it is also an issue for human health as well.' We criticise any attempt to stop trade in Eastern Europe and Spain, but our own hands are not entirely clean.

Fashion in riding styles is also very noticeable. Perhaps the most obvious is the rigid schooling typical of the dressage arena, with the horse's neck exaggeratedly flexed, but it is also apparent in show jumping. Peter Robeson, the British Olympic medallist in both the 1956 and 1964 Games, used to come into the arena at the London Horse Show riding with thick, white cord reins. He would rein his horse back to remind the horse that he was in charge and then set off totally unhurried. It would madden the Show Director, Colonel Ansell. Although blind, he was told precisely what was happening and he knew it was playing havoc with his schedule. I recall a moment at the White City, just as a major competition approached the final jump off with famous horses involved, when the Colonel turn to Dorian Williams, the well-known BBC commentator, and a master of letting the pictures tell their own story. 'Their (TV) time is up!' he roared. 'They must pay more for the jump off!' The BBC did not, of course, and we needed the publicity too. Sadly, I think the advent of too much sponsorship – Everest Forever, Sanyo Olympic Video or Next Milton – while undoubtedly helping the riders' expenses, soon proved to be an advertisement too far for the BBC and public, who may have longed for the simplicity of the likes of Marion (Coakes) Mould's pony, Stroller. Today, most horse shows are difficult to find in the main TV schedules. The Christmas Show at Olympia, of which I became chairman in 2001, is a very popular exception.

Extreme flexion, where the horse's head is encouraged or pulled down to his chest, often with draw reins, has long since been adopted from the dressage arena by show jumpers, but there is a line between what a horse wants to do naturally and comfortably and hyperflexion or *Rollkur*, which is banned by the FEI. A deep outline is one thing, unnatural behaviour is another, and I have noticed some trying to achieve the desired result without, I suspect, any real knowledge of what they are doing. I witnessed the same unnatural behaviour - or, should I say, exaggerated action - among hackney horses when, in later life, I became President of the Hackney Horse Society, whose members were great supporters of the South of England Show where their annual gathering has been held since 1967. Stewards were very much on their guard there because we used to have a certain amount of trouble with the hackney drivers from Belgium and Holland, who could be extremely rough with their horses.

Thanks to the strict rules covering international competition and riders, the FEI has managed to impose an international standard, and there is no doubt that professional competition, wherever it takes place and no matter who is involved, does not escape its scrutiny. In 2009, Sheikh Mohammed bin Rashid Al Maktoum, the ruler of Dubai and a dominant force in British horse racing, was banned for six months by the FEI from the increasingly popular endurance riding, after a horse he had been riding tested positive for a steroid. His wife, HRH Princess Haya of Jordan, was the FEI President at the time and a leading campaigner for a cleaner sport. She played a proactive role as president and it would be a mistake to think of her as just a well-connected figurehead. As a former member of the Jordanian Olympic show jumping team, she had first-hand knowledge of the sport and, whenever I attended FEI meetings on behalf of WHW, was extremely effective and spoke well; I was delighted to be able to introduce her to the work of WHW, as it is critical that all in horse sport should be aware of what is happening to equines around the world. As a result, Princess Haya has helped us to promote the charity whenever possible in the UK and on her travels. It came as a surprise to the sport and a personal sadness to me when she announced in August 2014 that she would not be seeking a third term as FEI President, citing personal reasons for her decision. She was succeeded by Ingmar De Vos of Belgium, who was Secretary General of the FEI.

In 2014, a 27-month doping ban was handed down to another prominent figure, Sheikh Hazza bin Sultan bin Zayed Al Nayan, a member of the Abu Dhabi ruling family, when, some two years after winning the President's Cup in 2012, his horse tested positive to the opioid analgesic propoxyphene. The delay was not explained. The drug was contained in Fustex, a booster, given to the horse the day before that 100-mile race. Three months were added to the usual two-year ban because Sheikh Hazza had been banned before, when his horse, Hachim, tested positive to an anti-inflammatory drug after winning the World Championship in 2005.

Endurance riding is a sport covering stretches of up to 80, 120 or 160 kilometres, with regular veterinary inspections along the way to check that horses are still sound. It was recognised as a formal sport in 1955 when Wendell Robie and some colleagues rode across the Sierra Nevada from Lake Tahoe to Auburn in a day. The Arabian breed is considered among the best for this sport because of its strength and stamina.

The problem is that money talks. The FEI can scrutinise as much as it likes, but it does not have a grip on countries which are not prepared to play by the rules or perhaps even regard our standards of horse welfare as soft. The Federation can hold enquiries at their headquarters in Lausanne but the nations most likely to be offending do not bother to attend. What sanctions are available? Suspension, financial penalty, a total ban? The first is just inconvenient and the last two are risible and unlikely to be imposed. The wealth of these nations means that they would barely even notice a fine, while a total ban cannot realistically be imposed on sovereign states which themselves run many of the events and offer tempting prize money. The FEI did impose an 'indeterminate suspension' to the UAE in March 2015 following continued offences in endurance riding.

Concern for the welfare of horses in endurance racing led to the establishment by the FEI of a task force charged with cleaning up the sport. There was some embarrassment in April 2014 when two of Sheikh Mohammed's senior employees, having been offered a significant role in the study, had to stand down and Sheikh Mohammed withdrew his offer to fund the clean-up. The Dutch and Swiss federations criticised their involvement, saying: 'Even if His Highness Sheikh Mohammed is the current endurance champion, his six-month suspension for using prohibited substances (in 2009) cannot be denied, not mentioning more than 24 positive cases concerning horses from his stables in past years.' (*Daily Telegraph*, 16 April 2014). A subsequent enquiry by the former Metropolitan Police Commissioner, Lord Stevens, cleared Sheikh Mohammed of having any personal knowledge of the 24 cases.

The murmurings of suspicion, provoked by this case and by imputations of sharp practice in endurance riding, should in fairness be countered by the obvious interest which Sheikh Mohammed shows in all his animals – camels and hawks as well as horses. Mary Bromiley, a pioneer of physiotherapy in the treatment of injured animals, wrote in her book, *A Way of Life*: 'I know he (Sheikh Mohammed) is sympathetic because I have witnessed it: if a horse falters during a ride he dismounts and he leads it in to the next check point despite the personnel travelling in a fleet of accompanying vehicles....Many accuse Sheikh Mohammed of only wanting to win, I would dispute this, in my experience he is a man who cares deeply for his animals and will go to all lengths to ensure the health, welfare and comfort of those he owns, no matter what this takes.'

The question remains: does the FEI have the teeth to police and deliver effective penalties in all the different elements of equestrian sport? And if it does not, what should be done to strengthen its authority? My impression is that the regulatory bodies are struggling to match the ingenuity of illegal science and that, as the prize money increases, so the temptation to take a risk will prove too great.

In June 2014, the FEI introduced new rules to tighten up on welfare issues in international endurance events including, crucially, extended rest periods as well as increased accountability for riders. Brian Sheahan, FEI chairman, said: 'This is a great step forward for horse welfare and fair play.' (*Horse and Hound*, 19 June 2014)

But concerns persist. No sooner had the FEI announced its tougher rules and sanctions then five top French vets wrote an open letter warning of what they called 'excesses' in endurance racing spreading to Europe. They said that at Compiègne CEI in May, where L'Emerita di Gallura, a Maktoum-owned horse, had died, the vets had '...*worked constantly under pressure from some competitors dealing with cheating and making challenging judgments. Then the treatment team had to deal with too many horses eliminated for metabolic reason with high heart rates and states of dehydration that were surprising given the mild weather of the weekend...Unfortunately the development of doping techniques can significantly disrupt conventional signs of fatigue that would normally alert us, so much so, that these practices will allow unsportsmanlike people with tired horses to stand at the vet gate with seemingly good reviews to even the most seasoned vet who must judge in a minimum time on a small number of clinical criteria.*'

The vets, including Jean-Louis Leclerc, a highly respected member of the Endurance Strategic Planning Group, said: '*These horses are put in grave danger by these cheating practices, which are unacceptable to us, as they are for any participant in these races, and we deplore this situation as it makes us cynical about the sport. They go completely against the spirit of sport and must be combated with pugnacity. Unfortunately, the complexity of detecting certain substances and cost make this prevention difficult. It does not take much to be defeatist or to leave the field open to those who are responsible for endangering these generous and exceptional horses, just for their own pride.*' (The co-signatories of the open letter, alongside Leclerc, were vets Christophe Pelissier, Pierre Romantzoff, Antoine Seguin and Benamou Agnes Smith).

It is impossible to point the finger of blame in these cases, but perhaps the pressure on staff is as much about not losing as it is about winning. Winning may mean anything from a house, a car or another Rolex; losing may mean taking the next boat home.

So much for riding at the highest level: how do young people get started and how do they know they are getting the best advice? Many schools and most instructors should be approved by the British Horse Society (BHS) who carry out regular inspections. This is also a safeguard for the welfare of horses in a yard. A parent wants to know not only that their child is going to receive regular proper instruction, rather than be used as just another pair of hands to muck out stables for no wages, but also that the horses their children might ride are sound and safe.

I can easily understand how someone wants to work with horses and care for them but, as we have seen, it can easily slip into neglect, perhaps through ignorance or an inability to say no when offered yet another rescue case. There are undoubtedly more horses than knowledgeable owners these days. One can see it out in the hunting field and at shows, where riders do not know how to manage their animals, do not know how to turn them out properly for events and, worse, do not even seem to care. Let's hope that the sight of another horse, properly plaited or wearing the appropriate tack, correctly fitted, will teach them something, even if it's only to ask what they should be doing better; this is, after all, where the professional riders of the future all start, attending local gymkhana events and hoping to progress. It is also where good and bad habits are picked up. When Raimondo d'Inzeo was watching his father instruct, he was lucky enough to get the best advice and went on to become a great show jumping star. Most importantly, though, he learned how to get the best out of his horses, and it was not by means of cruelty or by bending the rules to 'break' a horse.

By 1963, I had qualified as a solicitor and would soon be involved in the high-profile and most litigious and rule-ridden world of racing. The jockeys who compete are among the finest horsemen and women in the world, riding valuable horses for very high rewards. The difference between winning and losing can quite literally come down to the line. The questions then asked revolve around whether victory was fairly achieved or whether the rider has breached the rules of racing. The decision lies with the racing stewards of the day. If in doubt, my advice was always to 'hold an enquiry.'

3 | AT THE RACES

Is horse racing inherently cruel? Are we racing enthusiasts, from the occasional punter to the top-flight trainers and jockeys, not to mention Her Majesty the Queen, all culpable in one of the longest ever acts of continuous mistreatment of animals for pleasure and profit?

The first flat racing in England was recorded in 1174 at Smithfield in London. Both the United Kingdom and Ireland have been captivated by the pursuit of the perfect racehorse since the first Thoroughbred descendants of Byerly Turk, Darley Arabian and the Godolphin Arabian began arriving in the 17th and 18th centuries. To be recognised as a Thoroughbred with a capital T, the line has to be traced back to one of these three stallions. Descendants can now be found all over the world. Horse racing is regarded as the sport of kings, but perhaps it is not that exclusive a club any longer, with more than 100,000 foals registered worldwide each year.

That, some argue, is part of the problem. Such a proliferation of horses must mean that the majority will fail to make the grade, or at the very least will not be winners, and their lot is to be turned into dog meat – or even meat for human consumption - after a very short life. I have seen one report which claimed that 25,000 are destroyed every year: to me, that seems like a high number but probably many do suffer this fate simply because they cannot all be winners. It is as though the breeders and the owners are trying to improve their odds just by increasing the numbers. There is something sad about the fact that many young horses are not even named until they have proved themselves, because the big racing yards may want to keep their best names for what they hope will turn out to be their best horses.

It is an expensive business training horses; just witness the number of racing yards which struggle to keep afloat. Even the late, great Sir Henry Cecil had lows as well as highs before ending a glorious career with the unbeaten Frankel. Winners on that scale, though, earning their owners hundreds of thousands of pounds per race and even more in potential stud fees, are rare; for the most part, trainers have to be content with picking up small prize money of between £2,000–£3,000. Even those like John Dunlop who have served the industry faithfully for years, with 3,500 winners and ten Classics, including two Derby winners, are not spared when success eludes them; he was forced to put his stables into voluntary liquidation and end nearly half a century of training at the close of the flat racing season in November 2012. The horses, the owners or just the luck slipped away. Sad, too, are the knock-on consequences: what happens to the food supplier, the farrier, the staff, many of whom would no doubt have been in tied houses attached to the Duke of Norfolk's estate in Arundel where John had been the private trainer before getting his public licence.

With the 2008 recession, the number of racehorses fell as the economic downturn took hold, affecting the racing industry as it did every other business. Nevertheless, with 14,000 horses registered to race in Britain in 2013, it really does seem to be a numbers game.

It is all very well if there is a star performer in the yard, but generally a trainer needs at least 60 horses to make serious money as many will be off the road for one reason or another at time, or simply not be good enough. With fewer horses, major financial backing is needed to fund the lean seasons while the next winner is being trained. No wins, and the owners very soon start deserting your stable.

So where is the cruelty? The argument is that racehorses are trained and primed to run at such a speed that some bleed in their windpipes and their lungs; fed on a high protein diet, rather than grazing peacefully in a meadow, they develop stomach ulcers; and they race as two and three-year olds, before their bones and ligaments have had time to form fully. Critics point to the big prize money in the two year old races such as the Magic Millions Gold Coast Classic in Queensland, with $A2 million at stake, and the multi-million dollar events now being staged in Dubai. Maybe it is simply a case of economics: it's far cheaper for an owner to race a two year old than spend another 12 months waiting for a three year old, even if it may take another three years for the horse's skeleton to be fully formed. What was once an idle pastime for a few has now become a major money spinner and, some argue, at the expense of the horse's welfare. What should be done? Scrap all racing for two year olds? That is unlikely, not least because of the impact on huge investments and the risk to thousands of jobs; racing is worth some £3.4 billion, providing 17,500 full-time jobs as well as a further 67,500 indirect posts in the UK alone. But then how do we answer the charge that we are deliberately racing young horses, many of which are not physically able to take the strain? Champion trainer Martin Pipe, 'by an incalculable distance the pre-eminent trainer of his generation', to quote Alastair Down of *Racing Post*, gave me his down-to-earth opinion on the subject: 'Two year olds are bred to race at that age. Leaving them longer is like trying to teach a 15-year-old child good manners – impossible.'

The consensus veterinary argument may be put simply: just as some young-sters are not developed enough to play contact sports like rugby, so too some young horses are not up to the stresses and strains of racing. On the other hand, some undoubtedly are – one only has to watch a school rugby match today to see how much has changed. What has to be judged by trainers is which of the horses in their yards are up to the challenge. It all goes wrong when owners put pressure on the trainers to run horses when they are not ready or the ground is not right. As usual, it comes down to money – trainers who can pick and choose which horses and owners they allow into their yards will most probably make the right decision. Those starting out or with a modest string of horses might be tempted to have a go and hope for the best. And even if you have a good two-year old winner, the temptation is to cash in on that success and send it off to stud rather than risk its reputation being damaged as a three-year old. Fortunately most owners are pre-pared to continue racing.

Let's be frank: there is wrongdoing in the industry and there always has been. As I sit reading my *Racing Post*, the headlines speak yet again of illegal drug and anabolic steroid abuse, all presumably designed to speed up the healing process and strengthen muscles to gain an unfair advantage.

The hugely successful Godolphin stable at Newmarket was shaken in April 2013 when the BHA found that 11 horses, all trained by Mahmood Al Zarooni for Sheikh Mohammed, had tested positive for steroids. Al Zarooni was subsequently banned for eight years although Sheikh Mohammed, who was cleared of any involvement in or knowledge of the abuse, said that as far as he was concerned, as his employer, Al Zarooni was banned for life.

Then there is the blatant cruelty of administering electric shocks when the horse is wearing blinkers so that it associates blinkers with fear at the racecourse and runs faster. Sharp prods and pins are surreptitiously and illegally employed for the same effect or even, as we have seen in endurance racing in the Middle East, someone blatantly runs behind a horse cracking a whip to urge it on. Sheikh Mohammed bin Mubarak Al Khalifa was shown a 'yellow card' and fined $560 (£330) by the FEI for abuse of his winning horse, Tarabic Carl, in the King's Cup 120 km race at Sakhir, Bahrain in February 2014. A video went viral on the internet showing a man running behind, beating the horse, and another clip showed the rider whipping the horse with exceptionally long reins, contrary to FEI rules. The former editor of *Horse and Hound*, Lucy Higginson, and *Daily Telegraph* writer Pippa Cuckson protested that the yellow card was insufficient. The FEI subsequently upheld the protest, saying the sheikh should have been suspended. Apparently learning nothing, Sheikh Mohammed was given another yellow card on 23 May 2014 for 'abuse of a horse' and was automatically suspended for two months. However, it is hard to see how a $560 fine is likely to be any sort of deterrent in these cases.

Drug taking in all top class sport is with us to stay, so our only defence against it is to be cleverer than the abusers. The various authorities must also consider harsher penalties, both for the sake of the horses and for the good of the sport. As the racing correspondent Paul Hayward wrote: 'Racing needs trainers and owners to keep pressure on the authorities to act against those who think it acceptable to risk the health and lives of racehorses.' (*Daily Telegraph*, 6 March 2014).

In June 2014 the BHA announced that it was going to introduce a zero-tolerance policy towards anabolic steroids. From the New Year, any horse testing positive would be stood down immediately for 12 months and face a 14-month ban from racing in Britain. Significantly, imported horses would have to be registered within three months of arriving in Britain and registration would require a sample. Horses from Ireland, France and Germany would be treated as British horses because of their mirror policies with British racing. Even though there is a more lenient standard in America and South America, British trainers sending horses to race abroad would still have to stick to the British standard. The changes followed a review by Professor Sandy Love of Glasgow University following the Al Zarooni case. Paul Bittar, then Chief Executive of the BHA (he stood down in 2015), said: 'It is intended to ensure that the industry, racing and betting public can be reassured that all races which take place on British soil are on a level playing field.' (*Daily Telegraph*, 27 June 2014).

My reaction is that while it is a step in the right direction, the ban should be for life. No one can say definitively that a horse, its musculature, speed or even breathing have not been enhanced by illegal drugs. There should be no second chances. And yet the offences keep coming. In October 2014 the Irish trainer, Philip Fenton, was found guilty of eight drugs charges, including the possession of steroids and other banned substances. The drugs, including the anabolic steroid Nitrotain, which builds up muscle mass and improves stamina, and Ilium Stanabolic, sufficient for 250 doses, were found hidden under a horse rug next to a medicine store. Fenton, winner of the Hennessy Gold Cup at Leopardstown in 2014 with Last Instalment, was fined £4,780. At the hearing in Carrick-on-Suir, Co. Tipperary, the judge, Timothy Lucey, said of the offence and penalties: 'I think it's sufficiently serious that fines have to be such that other people won't be inclined to take liberties.' (*Daily Telegraph*, 24 October 2014). Maybe, maybe not, but the biggest penalty will always be the loss of good horses from a yard when owners disapprove. The Irish Turf Club followed up the fine in November 2014 with its own three-year suspension, disqualifying Fenton from all racing environments.

It is a worldwide problem. The *New York Times* conducted its own investigation in 2012 into the abuse of drugs to mask pain or stimulate performance in horses and reported a widespread drug culture among owners and trainers, aided and abetted by vets. They claimed that 24 horses died every week at American racetracks. The penalties, when offenders are caught, seem to be easily circumvented. The second-highest ranking US trainer, Steve Asmussen, with more than 6,700 winners and $214 million in prize money to his name, was given a six-month suspension in 2006 when a filly he was training tested 750 times over the legal limit for mepivacaine, a local anaesthetic used to kill pain. He simply handed the training duties over to his assistant, Scott Blasi, and his stables went on to rack up $14 million in earnings for the year. This sidestep would not be quite so simple in Great Britain, since an assistant trainer would need to obtain a licence from the BHA before any horse could run.

In 2014, following an undercover operation, Asmussen was again publicly accused of mistreating his horses by the People for the Ethical Treatment of Animals (PETA), long- standing opponents of thoroughbred racing. Without waiting for the outcome of enquiries by the New York Gaming Commission and the Kentucky Horse Racing Commission, the Egyptian owner, Ahmed Zayat, announced that he would immediately transfer his 12 horses out of Asmussen's yard. Zayat took offence when he saw the way in which one of his horses, Nehro, had been treated in the undercover video. The horse was in pain from sore feet but was kept in training until he died from colic. Asmussen was a finalist for the National Museum of Racing's Hall of Fame in March 2014 but was quickly removed from the final ballot when the story broke.

His first action was to fire Scott Blasi, who was heard in the secret video talking about electric 'buzzers' to make the horses run faster and pain-deadening treatment known as shock-wave therapy, as well as using profanity in describing an owner. The media then wanted to know if two Asmussen-trained favourites, Untapable and Tapiture, would be permitted to run in the Kentucky Oaks and Kentucky Derby respectively; critics said to do so might be seen as a failure by the industry to shake off the bad old ways. Commentators began asking if US racing would ever be able to reform itself and start winning the fans back to the tracks. The former chairman of the Jockey Club in America, Ogden 'Dinny' Mills Phipps, said there was 'a dark cloud hovering over our sport' and the fear was that Asmussen would be filmed by the world's media holding aloft a trophy.

Asmussen's response on NBC to Ogden Phipps' comments was: 'Very disappointing. I wish he would read over the actual allegations.' As for the allegation made against him by PETA, he said: 'It's misleading, untrue, and completely false. If you read the complaint, there's not one actual rule violation. The most bothersome thing about this is for anybody to think I'm not a good caregiver (to horses).'

As for PETA, it makes no secret of its dislike of the sport. Its Vice President, Kathy Guillermo, speaking to *USA Today*, said: 'PETA is an abolitionist organization. We don't believe animals should be exploited.'

In the event, both horses ran, Untapable pulled off a resounding victory in the Oaks and Asmussen did indeed lift the winner's trophy. Four months later, Asmussen re-hired Blasi, letting it be known that he thought Blasi had been punished enough. He said: 'I'm better with him... The barn is better with him... We work well together and are able to do more. You can't do it without the horses. It requires great help to take care of great horses.' (*Courier Journal*, 29 July 2014).

For the defence, as it were, there was nothing in the PETA documentary that implicated Asmussen. For the prosecution, the argument was that Blasi would not have done anything without Asmussen's say-so. The Kentucky Horse Racing Commission (KHRC) enquiry cleared Asmussen and Blasi of all charges brought by PETA following the release of what the KHRC called a highly-edited online video.

While the two men were exonerated, the public perception was that racing generally in the United States was up to its old tricks. Those on the inside may have had one view, those on the outside simply assumed that widespread malpractice allegations confirmed their worst suspicions: the sport was corrupt.

And the talk of a level playing field? I wish it existed, but anecdotal evidence is that drug abuse is so widespread, and has been going on for so many decades, that there will always be those who cannot resist giving their horses a medical helping hand. A clear distinction, however, must be drawn between abuse and the highly sophisticated scientific research into legitimate ways of improving performance and breeding.

No country, it seems, is immune from the problem. Dene Stansall, who describes himself as a horse welfare consultant for the UK non-profit organisation Animal Aid, said his organisation was constantly monitoring British racing because 'We don't believe the regulator is independent enough to get to grips with various issues of concern to Animal Aid...the industry exists within a veiled cloak.' Robin Mounsey of the BHA responded by saying: 'We are proud of the high standards of care that exist within the sport and anyone who does not put the welfare of the horse first has no place within British racing.' (*The Guardian*, 25 March 2014).

The problem remains that people suspect something rotten in the world of racing; they believe that there is drug abuse, fixing and cheating, and that view is hard, if not impossible, to eradicate. The trainers, the jockeys and the breeders all protest their innocence – they very seldom attend an enquiry or admit they were at fault – and at the bottom of the pile is the horse. Its reputation is unfairly tarnished, even though it may be a brilliant racehorse. Purely because someone decided to inject a drug into its system, its achievements later in its career, if it has one, will always be questioned – and in my view, rightly so. When Encke, the St. Leger winner and the highest profile of the Godolphin horses banned after the 2013 Al Zarooni scandal, lined up in the following August to race in the Coutts Glorious Stakes at Goodwood, I, at least, wondered about the effect of his history. In the event, he was beaten into second place. Encke died on 14 October 2014 after sustaining an injury on the gallops.

Once a horse has been found to have drugs in its system, how long do they take to clear? If those drugs are used for muscle growth, even if the abuse stops, how can one tell whether the muscles are natural or drug enhanced? I know of one filly which was banned for six months and entered for the 1000 Guineas at Newmarket. The question mark will surely hang over her every performance – was it drug enhanced or was she clean, with the steroids now out of her system? Should we simply say that once a horse has been found to have been drugged in this way it should be banned for life? In the world of athletics they have decided that this is too harsh, but a racehorse's career is much shorter. The argument in favour of a lifetime ban is compelling and I was pleased to read in March 2014 that Paul Bittar seemed to agree, although a spokesman for the BHA let it be known that they were 'disappointed' with the interview. Make of that what you will.

The pressure for change will have to come from the paying public, who increasingly are finding alternative ways of spending their leisure time. Attendance can at best be described as flat – 1.9 million in 2011, 1.8 million in 2012 and 1.7 million in 2013 at Jockey Club-owned courses. If people don't like what they perceive to be ill treatment, they will stop going to the races. In the meantime, illegal practices will continue because big money is involved, so we must be alert to that possibility and stamp them out quickly. When I was invited to be a steward for the first time at Plumpton in 1966, I have no doubt that it was my legal background as much as my interest in horses which counted in my favour. The qualifications and training of amateur racecourse stewards are much more detailed now than when I began. As I saw it, my duties were to serve the welfare of the horse and ensure the proper conduct of racing on the day, rather than to act as a prosecutor, but having taken part in many a court case, I did have the ability to weigh arguments dispassionately.

In my experience, those seeking to get the best out of their horses, whether in racing, eventing or showing, do so out of an inordinate love for horses, but the pressure to get a winner and to earn prize money, not to mention the even bigger rewards from stud fees, is constant. With so much at stake there will always be those who are prepared to break the rules. The message seems to be that you are only as good as your last race, so races have to be entered as soon as the horses are believed to be fit and capable, or sometimes earlier than that.

At one stage I upset the late Toby Balding, who, among more than two thousand other successes, trained Grand National, Cheltenham Gold Cup and Champion Hurdle winners. He entered a horse which was on the road to recovery from a tendon injury. We in the stewards' box decided that the horse was a 'non-trier', under what was then Rule 151, and Toby freely admitted afterwards that he just wanted to give the horse a run to see how its rehabilitation was going. In other words, he never intended the jockey to push his horse too hard; he was gently nursing it back to full racing strength. That was all very well for the horse, but it is against the rules of racing – one cannot just give a horse 'a bit of a run out' because punters are placing bets hoping that the horse will win. 'Trying out' a horse is a surprisingly common practice, but hardly the work of someone who does not care for his animals. As a result of this, Malcolm Wallace and I went to two training areas, Lambourn and Catterick, to make this ruling perfectly clear. Several trainers were indignant but in the end accepted it.

Toby's story makes the point, I hope, that trainers and jockeys naturally want to win, but for the most part their first instinct is the welfare of the horse. People have to love horses to be involved at this level; in fact, I would say one has to love horses to be involved with them at any level. On the whole it is an expensive and demanding business.

I would go further and say that the horses love the business as well. Unless horses are prepared to play their part, and it is the part for which they are bred, they will not give of their best. One can see the zest with which those willing to compete attack a course. A couple of my horses are now in their twenties, but they only have to see that they are about to go out hunting and they are up on their toes, raring to go – they are genuinely and instinctively 'gee-ed up'. Some racehorses can win without seeming to try. How often have we seen horses romp home as clear winners, just eating up the ground, like Captain Chris, who effortlessly, by 19 lengths, won the Ascot Chase in February 2014 for his jockey, Richard Johnson? Don't tell me he wasn't enjoying himself. What a joy to ride a horse like that.

Sometimes it can be the jockeys who are charged with not trying, or 'schooling in public'. I had to give evidence against the then National Hunt champion jockey, John Francome, who was found to be not trying as hard as he might at Plumpton on 14 October 1975, when I was assisting the chairman of the raceday panel. The decision against him was upheld by the Jockey Club Disciplinary Committee, although in the interest of balance I should say that John denies the charge to this day.

Then there is the other extreme, where jockeys are perceived to be pushing too hard and making excessive use of the whip. Use of the whip will be covered in a later chapter, but this argument is as old as racing itself, and reams have been written about the subject. Jockeys know instinctively what a horse can and cannot do. In the past there was certainly excessive use of the whip on occasions but today, with the advent of comprehensive television coverage, the stewards and the general public simply do not tolerate the practice.

Jockeys themselves have contributed enormously to changes in the rules about use of the whip as well as in the design of the whip itself. A total ban on whips has rightly been rejected because, as any rider will know, it is an essential aid, particularly when riding in fast-moving groups of horses. Most riders also use a whip as a reminder to the horse to concentrate, for encouragement as well as an aid to steering.

The BHA's rules on the subject in 2014 were clear and put the welfare of the horse and the safety of the rider at the top of its priorities:

1. Showing the horse the whip and giving it time to respond before hitting it.
2. Using the whip in the backhand position for a reminder.
3. Having used the whip, giving the horse a chance to respond before using it again.
4. Keeping both hands on the reins when using the whip down the shoulder in the backhand position.
5. Using the whip in rhythm with the horse's stride and close to its side.
6. Swinging the whip to keep a horse running straight.

The BHA, which ultimately assumed all responsibilities for the conduct of horseracing from the Jockey Club in 2007, held a wide-ranging enquiry into the use of the whip as well as carrying out scientific studies into energy-absorbing whips and their effectiveness on horses. It concluded that there needed to be tougher penalties for abuse of the whip and introduced new rules about the frequency of using the whip, such as in the final furlong of a race. Horse welfare was its primary concern. Tougher penalties for abuse of the whip are an old chestnut and one which generally provokes a swift reaction from the leading jockeys: 'I can't believe a sport that tries to stop you from winning' – AP McCoy. 'Why can't we be allowed to practise our profession?' – Pat Eddery. (*Racing Post*, 12 January 1999)

The use and abuse of the whip was to become the most high profile topic during my tenure as chairman of the Jockey Club Disciplinary Committee. The argument, though, still rumbles on. After complaints from jockeys about the interpretation of new rules, the BHA eventually agreed that there should be flexibility rather than a rigid adherence to the number of times a whip was used, which prompted the RSPCA to issue a statement calling the BHA's U-turn ' a black day for the racing industry.' Having watched countless races, I disagree. Jockeys know how to get the best out of their rides and, as I have noted, if horses do not want to race, they never will. Occasionally they simply refuse to join in at all, as poor Brendan Powell discovered in the 2014 Grand National, when Battle Group refused to start. The same horse played up again just over a week later in the *Coral Scottish National Handicap Steeple Chase* at Ayr on 12 April 2014, and Powell found himself facing a disciplinary enquiry for excessive use of the whip when the gelding initially proved unwilling to start. The Disciplinary Panel found him in breach of the rules for the frequency and rapidity of his use of the whip and he was suspended for five days.

Some will never agree with the argument for whips. I was interviewed on this subject by the ebullient TV racing pundit, John McCririck, on Channel 4's The Morning Line. He was almost vitriolic in his questioning as he believed that whips were unnecessary. It wasn't just for the cameras, because after the interview he continued, prodding me in the chest to make his case. He was very passionate about it and although I was impressed that he was not just giving a performance for the viewers, I have not changed my mind. His wife, Jenny, is very supportive of World Horse Welfare. Love him or hate him, John McCririck, while being unpredictable, was passionate about his racing and when he was unceremoniously dumped by Channel 4, something of that passion was lost from the coverage. After his dismissal, he didn't gloat in interviews at falling viewing figures for the programme; he was, instead, concerned. 'The trouble is too many of the people making decisions there don't like betting. If they could have racing without betting they'd do it, but the viewers clearly don't agree,' he said (*Racing Post*, 29 June 2014). TV punditry today, though, demands professional sports personalities and it is unlikely that McCririck would ever have been able to master the electronic wizardry of touch screens in order instantly to replay action in quite the same way as Frankie Dettori, who became a new and deft operator on The Morning Line in 2014.

All, however, would agree that hitting a slow horse will not turn it into a fast horse, nor will kicking it in the side with spurs. At the most junior level of riding in the Pony Club there are rules about children wearing spurs in events and they have to be approved to wear them in competitions by their branch's District Commissioners. Junior riders with aspirations to progress to professional levels are rightly being taught to put their ponies first and winning second.

I would totally refute the suggestion that jockeys are simply driving their horses harder and harder, regardless of their wellbeing. These are highly skilful horsemen and women and they know when a horse is not trying and when it can do no more; many a time a jockey will pull up a horse which simply cannot cope with the pace and trot it back. Equally, a horse may refuse to go into the stalls or even refuse to come out of them. If they do that more than twice, they have to take a stalls' test to see if they are 'reformed characters' before they are allowed to be entered for another race.

Whether racehorses fail to make the grade, or simply get too old for the game, there comes a time when owners and trainers have to let them go. This is now recognised by the industry, which has established various charities for the retraining and rehoming of the thousands of racehorses that leave the sport every year. Charities like Retraining of Racehorses (RoR) are funded by donations from owners, racecourses, trainers, bookies and jockeys, among others. Thoroughbreds cannot simply give up racing one day and then be hacked out occasionally the next, or turned out into a field. It would be much kinder to put them down. They are like coiled springs and have to adapt over time to a gentler, slower pace of life. In January 2015 WHW, in collaboration with RoR, launched a pilot project at its centre in Norfolk to help prepare racehorses for a life away from the tracks.

In our recent experience at WHW, we no longer find many thoroughbreds languishing unloved and abandoned in fields, thanks in large part to the rehabilitation work of a number of charities. Occasionally horses find a potentially successful new career like Kauto Star, winner of the Cheltenham Gold Cup, which went on to compete successfully in dressage. This is the sort of encouraging and high profile example which we should salute. It comes back to repaying the horse for what it has delivered in its racing life and, increasingly, a share of the prize money in racing goes to charities to back the retraining of racehorses.

One of my early experiences as a steward at Plumpton, in August 1972, illustrates a point about jockeys' concern for horses; it was also an unnerving occasion for me as I found myself chairman of the stewards' panel for the first time that day – a Bank Holiday with a very large crowd. I was sitting with Captain Dicky Courage RN, incidentally the only naval officer to have won the Grand Military Gold Cup known as the Soldiers' Grand National. The stewards' paid secretary was with us, as usual, and he knew the rule book from cover to cover.

It was the first meeting of the season and five or six jockeys were booked to ride, including David Mould, at the time the Queen Mother's long-standing jockey. Having walked the course, the jockeys said they refused to ride because the fences were too stiff, having been newly-stuffed during the summer.

The secretary was quite adamant and said that if they wouldn't run 'we should send them all to London.' They could, in other words, be punished by a higher authority at the Jockey Club. At this point I got a kick under the table from Dicky, who was much older than me but had come to stewarding later in life.

I thanked the secretary for his advice and, after some discussion and with the agreement of the Clerk of the Course, who was anxious that a profitable day's racing should not be lost, suggested that, if the jockeys agreed to race, the racecourse would give an undertaking to modify the fences before the next meeting. That's what happened and the racing went ahead, although it did not stop the *Sporting Life* running a story: Jockeys Warn 'We'll Strike'.

The fences probably were a little stiff but at least I had previously walked the course with the clerk of the course, who probably thought they were fine, and I was basing my decision on what I had seen rather than what I had just heard. It was, though, the beginning of the jumping season and the last thing we wanted was fallen horses and injuries to jockeys who had already voiced their concerns. And that is the point: they were professionals, they knew precisely what the horses were capable of and, quite reasonably, they did not want to risk either the horses or themselves on firm ground at the start of the season. This was neither the action of callous people who did not have a care about their rides nor was it anything to do with fear – jump jockeys are a fearless bunch, who are prepared to take the knocks and the falls and get straight back into the saddle.

Racing is a hazardous sport and the question of fences is always going to be an issue. The Grand National is the race which attracts the most criticism, with calls every year, particularly after major pile-ups, for the jumps to be made easier. It is not just Aintree. In March 2014 at Cheltenham, falls on the opening two days of the Festival led to Our Conor, Akdam and Stack the Deck being put down. There were fears that we would be witnessing a repeat of 2012, when five horses died. Initial investigations suggested that Our Conor at least had fallen after making a mistake, but the RSPCA immediately launched an investigation, studying the course, the race and the number of runners in the field. Raya Star then had a terrible fall in the Grand Annual Steeple Chase and also had to be put down. The list of casualties was far too high. Jockeys, too, suffered major injuries. Paul Struthers, Chief Executive of the Professional Jockeys' Association said: 'For the sheer volume of very serious injury, it is the worst I have seen.' (*Daily Telegraph*, 17 March 2014).

Happily, there were no casualties the following month at the Aintree Grand National where the new design of the fences – a core made of flexible plastic rather than of wood - and improved irrigation have made a big difference. WHW would still like to see an experimental reduction in the size of the field because only 18 of the 40 runners made it round the four and a half miles and 30 fences. Roly Owers said: 'We are concerned at the relatively high number of fallers and unseated riders which pose safety risks to horses and their jockeys.' He wondered whether there should be a 'trial reduction' in the number of horses competing, although one of the attractions to many, who may only ever watch this one race in a year, is the very size of the field; according to Steve Harman, chairman of the BHA, 400 million people worldwide are said to watch the race every year (*Daily Telegraph*, 27 May 2014). At more than four miles over stiff fences, it will always be a challenge to horse and rider.

But Aintree is used to such dramas. The 1993 Grand National was declared void after a series of false starts, the first caused by protestors getting on to the course, followed by another two false starts when the horses became entangled in the starting gate. On the last occasion, the recall man failed to wave his red flag and seven of the jockeys completed the two circuits of the course. The 'winner' was Esha Ness, trained by Jenny Pitman and ridden by John White, but in reality it was the National that never was.

The stewards' responsibility is to ensure that it is safe to race and, once racing begins, to see that it is conducted fairly – although when I first started in 1966 there were few cameras monitoring events, apart from one looking down the finishing straight to check that there was no interference. We had to rely on following the race through our binoculars and on our common sense and racing experience.

The only people who can call a race off are the stewards. I would argue that they have a duty of care to the jockeys and their horses in equal measure. The rules are changing and whereas in the past there would be just one professional official – the secretary – advising the three stewards, who were unpaid amateurs, today there are two professionals and two amateurs. I regret this because when there is a difference of opinion, it is quite likely that the professionals who go racing most days will get their way and it will be much harder for the unpaid hands, who perhaps go racing only once a fortnight, to make their voices heard. From a legalistic point of view, I can foresee conflicts arising because the professionals are increasingly ex-jockeys and there may be 'history' between some past and present riders.

There is nothing new about the concept of professional stewards. 'Monkey' Blacker was asked to conduct an enquiry into the idea on behalf of the Jockey Club in the early 1980s. His findings, having interviewed some 100 witnesses and being quite prepared to recommend the professional route, surprised him: 'The great majority, including jockeys and trainers with experience of racing overseas, firmly upheld the amateur system as being fairer and more even-handed than a professional one,' he wrote in his memoir *Monkey Business* (Quiller Press). The pool then was sufficiently robust, honest and capable of doing the job, although a cull of those doing it just as a social perk, particularly of chairmen who had landed the job through 'Buggins' turn', was carried out. I believe we must still have a big enough pool of potential amateur stewards with sufficient strength of personality to do the job, or the leadership ability that derives from commanding men and women in battle or in the boardroom, combined with a knowledge and passion for horses.

The role of the steward, much like a referee in a rugby match, is to ensure that the day's racing runs smoothly. The training of stewards is taken very seriously and all have to attend an annual refresher training session if they wish to act. There have been occasions when stewards appeared to be too high-handed – on one infamous occasion, a steward gave a Channel 4 racing producer a dressing down, refusing to let him sit down at a meeting and ordering him to take his hands out of his pockets as if he were a naughty schoolboy. The press loved it, especially when a photograph was published the next day of that steward arriving with his hands in his pockets.

The duty of care is terribly important. Jockeys are aware of this but occasionally they can fall foul of the rules. Sometimes, too, they try and use them to their advantage. In 1997, for example, Frankie Dettori was riding at Southwell. He was and remains a star, having ridden all seven winners at Ascot in September the previous year and countless other top races. My predecessor, Anthony Mildmay White, had introduced a totting up system, much like motoring penalty points, for infringements such as careless riding or excessive use of the whip, so that if a jockey had been stood down for a total of eight days they would automatically be banned from riding for a statutory two weeks. This penalty still exists.

On this occasion Frankie was on the verge of being stood down, having accumulated a number of 'points' and was blatantly waving his whip around. It was clear that he wanted to be stood down: there were no important races in the near future and we guessed he wanted a two-week break.

As we didn't have to suspend him at once, we thought we would impose a penalty at a time when it was really inconvenient for him. I knew that he wanted to ride in the Japan Cup in 1997, then the richest race in the world, so we agreed to suspend him so that he would miss that race.

A short time later, I found myself in Hong Kong proposing a toast to racing at the Carbine Club lunch. I happened to be sitting next to the champion Australian jockey, Darren Beadman, who had just announced his retirement in favour of a career in the Church, although I think he must have had second thoughts, because I later saw him riding again. Plenty of drink was flowing and I decided afterwards to go down to the sauna and sweat some of the alcohol out. I was sitting there, naked and undefended, my head in my hands, when in walked Frankie. 'I am sorry about the Japan Cup,' I said, but he just laughed it off. 'That's racing,' he replied and we went on to talk about the number of rides he was taking. I suggested that, with his undoubted talent, he should be more sparing with his time and I noted that a month or two later he told the press that he was going to be more selective and not chase the Champion Jockey prize, which goes to the rider with the most winners. Jockeys are under pressure to accept rides whenever they are offered, and that is seven days a week. As an aside, there is excellent racing in France on a Sunday, but generally speaking the quality available in the UK on Sunday is poor and the BHA should be offering less but better racing on a Sunday.

So on the serious point, yes: cruelty certainly does exist in the equestrian world, but horses love to run, even out-run one another. It is their instinct and what they have been bred to do. When a jockey falls, his horse, more often than not, will carry on racing and even jumping until the opportunity presents itself for him to run out. So no, horseracing is not inherently cruel, but pushing a horse artificially through the use of drugs or other stimulants is to be condemned. Unlike an athlete, who can make a decision as to whether or not to cheat, a horse takes what he is given.

The racing industry will never be prepared to wait until a horse is five years old before it can start racing. Horseracing is a multi-billion dollar business and to that extent it is harsh. Investors are looking for a quick return on their money by the time a horse is three, when its real earning potential can be realised by using it in stud for breeding. Prices are high: at the Inglis Easter yearling sales in Sydney in April 2014, the Emirates Park and Sheikh Mohammed bin Khalifa Al Maktoum partnership paid $1.5 million for a Street Cry colt.

Not all horses are winners and their 'careers' are relatively short, but I am certain that when they are racing – not being pushed, not being doped, not being beaten for lack of effort – then they are happy, indeed eagerly waiting for the next chance to go out and run. It is hard to imagine any other domesticated animal being better looked after than a racehorse when it is in training.

About this time, I was also becoming more involved as a solicitor and former Hunt Chairman in the administrative side of fox hunting, so it now seems appropriate to address the apparent contradiction of a man who cares deeply about the welfare of animals, while at the same time being a lifelong supporter of fox hunting.

I was appointed legal adviser to the Master of Foxhunting Association (MFHA) in 1983 and, contrary to what many might imagine, our time was not taken up by the threat to hunting, but by managing the internal affairs of the various hunts up and down the country. My own local hunt, the Eridge, had had to manage the dismissal of our huntsman. Captain Ronnie Wallace was chairman of the MFHA and regarded as God in the hunting world; he hunted frequently, six days a week, and was reputed to have an innate understanding of the ways of the fox. He had suggested that we were making a mistake about dismissing our huntsman, but I disagreed and even slammed the phone down on him when he suggested we could discuss the matter further on Christmas Day – I had better things to do. Some time later I heard via Edward Cazalet, who became a High Court judge, that Ronnie wanted to speak to me again. I was dismissive until Edward told me that Ronnie just wanted to ask me to become legal adviser to the MFHA.

I see no contradiction in my support both of WHW and of hunting and my position is succinctly put in this extract from the *Daily Telegraph* leader column (23 December 1996), when the country was vigorously debating the pros and cons of a ban on hunting foxes with hounds.

'The intellectual case against hunting is full of holes. More foxes are shot or snared than are hunted with hounds, and their death is more painful than the instantaneous elimination of those overtaken by the pack. A hunting ban would not lead to foxes being left alone; farmers, who regard them as vermin, would merely resort to crueller, legal methods of eradication. In most of the rest of Europe, which lacks a foxhunting tradition, the animals have been shot and snared almost to extinction. Is this what the saboteurs want?'

No amount of reasoned argument will persuade the determined hunt saboteurs, so there is little that can be said here to convince them. But I have lived in the country all my life, I have been surrounded by farmers who have seen what a rampant fox population can do and I have no doubt that hunting is the swiftest and most efficient way of managing them.

Farmers do not want to eradicate foxes, and neither does any real countryman but, just like deer, they need to be controlled, albeit for different reasons. A study in the Journal of Wildlife Management in 2013 said 750,000 deer need to be culled each year just to keep their numbers under control, to protect woodland and the bird population. The management of the countryside has to be taken in the round. Whatever we do will have an immediate impact somewhere. Take as an example the decision made many years ago by someone, in their wisdom, that because fencing had been wrecked by the 1987 hurricane, a managed herd of red deer in East Sussex should be destroyed rather than be allowed to roam free. However, red, fallow and roe deer as well as muntjac have bred and are now considered to be vermin and out of control. There are also deer on the islands in Scotland which will simply die of starvation if they are not regularly culled, because they are stripping away all the vegetation. Is it kinder to keep the numbers down or let nature take its cruel course?

For years farmers have ensured there were coppices where they knew foxes would breed, which meant their population could be controlled by local hunts.

Without hunting and without management of the land in this way, maybe because a new landowner opposes hunting, there has already been an increase in the number of foxes. They are now spreading into the urban environment as are deer, which have been photographed wandering the towns looking for suitable gardens on which to graze. The landscape itself will change in time.

There is always a knock-on effect from any change in the countryside but there can also be benefits. The huge sums of money poured into the breeding of racehorses have a trickledown effect throughout the equestrian world, and it is important that the right sort of breeding takes place. At the other extreme which we in WHW encounter is the wrong sort of breeding with no care and no science. It is that which leads to hundreds of horses and ponies being abandoned in fields and on roadsides because they have not made the grade.

Before I leave his chapter, here's a thought about Captain Ronnie Wallace which still makes me smile. With the onset of health and safety regulations, it was decided that those working with horses must wear a hard hat with a chin strap, as opposed to a cloth cap or similar. The Captain was incensed. 'We cannot have our huntsmen riding with a strap under their chins, they will look ridiculous and we must fight this!' I was asked to speak to Edward Cazalet who was prepared, without prevarication, to produce a legal opinion to the effect that a huntsman would not be able to blow his horn properly with the strap in place. There were certain exclusions allowed under the Act, but of course huntsmen were not excluded.

'What are you going to do now?' I asked the Captain. 'Go to the Home Office and get an exclusion, of course!' was the reply. 'Who will you see?' 'The Home Secretary, of course!' The exclusion was duly included.

1 | THE JOCKEY CLUB

The Jockey Club was formed in London in 1750 and has regularly been lampooned in the press as a club for rich toffs, a social club with no interest in the propriety and good management of horse racing. In fact, the Jockey Club has been a body of influence and a source of sustained investment in racing over a period spanning four centuries and is recognised as such worldwide. The Jockey Club Rooms in Newmarket have been at the heart of British racing virtually from the start, when King Charles I decided to put on a race there in 1622.

As the biggest organisation in British racing, the Jockey Club owns a large estate, including the two racecourses in Newmarket as well as the majority of the top racecourses in England, including Aintree, Cheltenham and Epsom. All profits (£22 million in 2013) are ploughed back into the sport. The Club was the regulator of all aspects of racing until its responsibilities were handed over in 2007 to the British Horseracing Board, later the British Horseracing Authority encompassing the Horseracing Regulatory Authority. The argument in large part for the change was the potential conflict of interest in the Club sitting in judgement as a major stakeholder on itself and its activities. The call seemed to be going out that it was time to become more professional.

Let us wind the clock back to 1990 when I was elected to the Jockey Club. I clearly recall walking twice round Portman Square in London, where it was then based, preparing myself for my first meeting. I felt very much like the new boy at school on his first day and yet I was now a senior partner in our law firm, had chaired many committees and had plenty of experience in the big wide world. What was there to be anxious about? I did not want to be late, but neither did I want to stand around with no one to talk to.

The Jockey Club had sole control of all racing in the country and stood as judge and jury on all its activities. It was impressive and awe-inspiring enough to put anyone on their mettle and I was right to be nervous, as so much depended on the Club's rulings. Yet it was and remains an organisation whose members give freely of their time precisely to ensure the well-being of the industry, despite the tone of commentaries in the press, particularly when there was a controversial Jockey Club ruling. Its members were for racing and all its practitioners, not against them. In short, the members cared deeply for the sport and carried out their duties without any expectation of reward or advancement. We had no axe to grind. We were amateurs in the strictest sense of the word, but the combined knowledge of racing in our meetings was considerable. It reminds me somewhat of the old unelected status of the House of Lords, where the Peers' independence and worldly experience were brought to bear in their scrutiny of government bills before the 'hereditaries' were replaced by so many political appointees. The old guard were in nobody's pocket. They could be relied upon to give a fair and honest opinion without worrying if they had offended anyone to whom they owed their position, thanks to political or even financial support. In the same way, we all felt we had an enormous responsibility to do right by racing. It was for that reason that I felt that a huge sense of personal privilege and real respect for the organisation to which I had been elected as I walked slowly round Portman Square on my first day.

I can already hear the cry go up: 'Self-elected!' In fact, you never knew who had put your name forward and the members could just as easily blackball you as accept the recommendation. But is that worse than any other system? Everyone who was elected to the Jockey Club had a long history of involvement in racing, which at the very least showed that they respected the sport and everything to do with it. Members were expected to help when asked and lend what expertise they had freely. This is hardly the activity of a group of people actively working against the sport and yet, if one reads some of the commentaries in the press at the time, one would have thought we were all involved in some elaborate Ponzi Scheme to fleece the punters.

There are four formal meetings a year for members of the Club. In 1990, we sat in a subterranean room in rows of high-backed chairs. The style of the meeting in those days was still very formal. The chairman was always addressed as 'Senior Steward' and when anyone asked a question they put their hand up but did not stand up, peering instead round the high-backed chair in front of them. It was ludicrous, really, and one of the innovations by Lord Hartington, now the Duke of Devonshire, in his time as Senior Steward, was the introduction of a huge oval table, making discussions so much easier.

The criticism that many of its members were rich enough to do all this on an unpaid basis, while being accurate, carried an unjustified insinuation that there was something exclusive and private about it, that we wanted to exclude all outsiders and somehow keep racing as the preserve of wealthy owners who patronised the leading trainers and the finest racing yards. In my experience, that simply never stood up to examination and my first 'blooding' in the club is an example.

In 1991, we were approached by the British Harness Racing Club to see if The Jockey Club would enter into some form of joint affiliation. In effect, they wanted the Jockey Club to govern their activities much as we ran thoroughbred racing. They wanted our blessing, our acceptance and perhaps even an imprimatur of respectability. I was asked to chair a study group and to come up with a recommendation. Harness racing, or trotting racing, was growing in popularity around the world and looked spectacular under lights; it was also profitable. Although evening betting had not started in the UK at that point, it was only a matter of time until it would be. When we were carrying out our study, the Pari Mutuel Urbain (or French Tote) reported a betting turnover of £3.5 billion in 1991, of which nearly half came from trotting.

As part of our investigation, we were invited to watch the racing in Sweden and France. The French fêted us and treated us to dinner in the Eiffel Tower; I suspect they were keen for British trainers to take on some of their less successful horses and they showed us their amazing training facilities in Paris.

I recall visiting a provincial track outside the city where they were mixing trotting with flat racing. We were rather late arriving for the huge lunch given beforehand, at which each region had brought their speciality. When we reached the speeches and the Calvados at the end there was a toast to "le Jockey Club". I did understand that and, in my best schoolboy French, thanked everyone: '*Toujours nous aimons nos chevaux.*' We also attended meetings at various places in the UK, including a farm near York and another near Bannockburn where interest was building, and Lingfield, which had tried mixing flat racing with trotting.

So things were beginning to happen in the UK and the questions were: did the Jockey Club want to become involved in what some of the purists in the racing world regarded as a sport of inferior quality. Were we being asked somehow to add a veneer of respectability to an area of horse racing best left alone? There were, and continue to be, stories about illegal trotting races, with substantial sums to be won, taking place at night on blocked-off A-roads. Indeed, the A27, which has a long straight stretch between Fontwell Park racecourse and Chichester, has a sign - No Trotting Racing - but continued in 2015 to be used illegally, early on Sunday mornings. This was hardly the sport of kings, but in places, notably America, it was a highly popular and professionally-run operation. In France, the *Prix d'Amérique*, the top harness race of the year, generates more revenue than the more prestigious and older Prix de l'Arc de Triomphe.

When I finally presented our study group's report to the Jockey Club in December 1992, there were already 230 trotting fixtures in the country, off-course betting was in full swing in Wales and there were plans to televise 25 meetings on local TV. On the face of it, we thought the sport was about to take off.

I faced a barrage of questions from the members of the Jockey Club. It was noted that some in the trotting race world could be a rough lot; others were concerned about diverting funds away from Flat and National Hunt thoroughbred racing, to the detriment of the equine industry as a whole. We were, in other words, alert to the possibility of expanding into other potentially lucrative avenues of racing and ready to embrace anyone with the good of racing at heart, while our focus was to preserve not some narrow clique, but the welfare of the horse and horse racing.

Our recommendation was that an affiliation should be established and this was agreed by the Jockey Club members, but in the end the British Harness Racing Club itself decided to go it alone. Some time later, they came back and asked us again if we would consider a link-up but we declined – the opportunity and the moment had passed. However, the sport endures in 2015 and we have a family of travellers at the end of our lane with trotters being exercised past us on a daily basis. Talking to one of the drivers recently, I asked about his horse which looked in very good condition. Proudly, he told me that it was a two-year-old and had just arrived from Australia!

King James I 'discovered' Newmarket on 28 February 1605 when he became lost during a hare course in Suffolk, realised that he had stumbled across ideal sporting country and moved his court there, much to the annoyance of his officers of state. He then commissioned the building of a palace. The first recorded race at Newmarket took place on 8 March 1622. King Charles I took to the sport of horse racing, regarding Newmarket as his second home, and spring and autumn meetings were established in 1627 while the king continued to conduct state business from the palace there. The Sport of Kings has been patronised by many of the monarchs of England, and the present queen, who is Patron of the Jockey Club, has enjoyed considerable success. She is both enthusiastic and knowledgeable about the sport, and her horses, which she has bred, have won many of the greatest races. The history of the Jockey Club is indeed steeped in the world of high society; the aristocracy were the only people at the time who could indulge in owning a racehorse, let alone a string of them. Today, though, there is nothing to stop anyone with just one good horse from entering and winning a race, although there are rules, qualifications and registration procedures.

Who dominates racing today? It is the Arab nations with their enormous financial resources and, among the jockeys, it is surely the Irish who seem to have a sublime gift when it comes to getting the best out of a horse. If anyone should doubt that, just witness the extraordinary ride and victory by 20-1 shot Lord Windermere, trained by Jim Culloty and ridden by Davy Russell in the Cheltenham Gold Cup in 2014. For most of the race, the horse was trailing towards the back of the field. Russell patiently coaxed him forward to win on the line by a minimal distance, beating On His Own. It was a planned race strategy but both Russell and Culloty looked mightily relieved when the stewards finished their ten-minute deliberation, as there had clearly been some interference by the winner. Culloty, who rode Best Mate to win that race three times in a row from 2002, had achieved the rare feat of winning the race as a trainer and a jockey.

Having a title may not give one a free pass to the winner's enclosure, but horse racing is an expensive business. When I was being quizzed about diverting the Jockey Club's efforts into harness racing, the real concern was that resources might be dissipated. They were at the time being poured into the racecourses, the National Stud - now owned by the Jockey Club - and welfare via our support for racing charities. This included Racing Welfare, supporting only stud and stable staff who work or have worked in British racing.

Another charge often laid at the door of the Jockey Club was that of incompetence. The problem, according to our critics, was that we were noting but bumbling amateurs who, because we were perceived to be merely dabbling in racing, could not possibly either understand it or regulate it properly. Examples were cited where the Jockey Club Disciplinary Committee had 'wrongly' overruled local stewards following an appeal, meaning that the owners or trainers had lost out.

Judging how a horse or a jockey has performed in a race is not an exact science; it can be a matter of opinion whether or not a horse has veered off course or was not trying, or whether a jockey had ridden illegally or just carelessly. Mistakes undoubtedly were and will continue to be made but are things so much better now? The ruling to have two professionals sitting with two 'amateur' stewards from the Jockey Club at race meetings, as I have noted, may actually have its drawbacks, and I wonder if we are seeing fewer offences in racing today, now that anyone tainted by their original association with the Jockey Club appears to be being gradually pruned from the BHA. Maybe I am being over-sensitive.

Racing has no doubt always been open to abuse, because extraordinary levels of money are involved for top races, top horses and top stud fees. Races are said to be fixed, horses doped and jockeys bribed. I do not believe matters have improved since the Jockey Club relinquished its authority following some arm-twisting by the government of the day, which did not like the fact that the Horserace Betting Levy Board, that had in part funded racing, was controlled by the Club. Lord Hartington led the vote as Senior Steward on handing authority over to the British Horseracing Board. He later recalled: 'We had been told by government in no uncertain terms that if racing wanted any sort of financial assistance, or even an ear, the sport could not be run by a completely undemocratic process.' (*Financial Times*, 15-16 December 2007).

Problems did occur in the past and, just as today, there were high-profile casualties, which incidentally go some way to disproving the notion that the old Jockey Club favoured the elite.

In December 1990, HRH The Aga Khan, whose horses won the English Derby three times during the 1980s, withdrew from British racing after his 1989 Oaks winner Aliysa was disqualified after testing positive for hydroxycamphor, a metabolite of the banned substance camphor. All hell broke loose and there followed an extremely complex series of hearings in the High Court in London. In the end the Aga Khan did not win the day. There was a lot of heartache and, for more than two years, we no longer saw the famous green colours with red epaulettes at British race meetings. Finally, in 1994, after the Jockey Club had improved its drug testing methods, Prince Karim announced that he was ending his boycott.

Some years later, when I had become chairman of the Jockey Club Disciplinary Committee, I went to Paris for the Prix de l'Arc de Triomphe, their biggest flat race. My wife and I were invited to their pre-race dinner, which they held the night before the race. After the meal, I saw the Aga Khan standing on his own, waiting for his coat. We had had great success at home with a horse called Nadjati, which had been bred and raced by the Aga Khan, but it was not up to his high standards and he had sold it. It came to England, ran over fences, initially enthusiastically, but got thoroughly bored being in a nose-to-tail racehorse string, so was sold to us at about the age of nine. We took Nadjati hunting, which rejuvenated him, and my son Philip won a series of point-to point and Hunter Chases with him. So that evening I introduced myself to the Aga Khan, just to tell him what a lot of fun we had had with his old horse. I said: 'My name is Christopher Hall. I am chairman of the Jockey Club Disciplinary Committee.' The Aga Khan looked momentarily shocked: 'My God,' he replied, 'what have I done wrong now?!'

I accept that the world has moved on, in the sense that everything requires formal regulation and governance, and people in positions of authority – particularly authority over substantial sums of money – have to be formally elected and seen to be answerable. Such controls are wise, I am sure, but at the same time I feel that something has been lost. The amateur stewards who nowadays sit with professional appointees, while having the casting vote at enquiries, have to have a very good reason to overrule the opinion of those professionals and inevitably, I believe, their long term position is under threat.

Today, the Jockey Club continues to manage its considerable portfolio of racecourses, training centres and breeding interests as it pursues its declared aim of making 'British horseracing the best in the world for the next 50 years and beyond.' At the very centre of everything it does and has ever done is the horse.

At the Jockey Club Rooms in Newmarket is a unique collection of artwork and mementoes dedicated to the real stars of the sport: the racehorses themselves. In the Stewards' Room, with its leather-lined sound-proofed walls, is a horseshoe-shaped table with three chairs behind it and a mat in front, where the offending trainer or jockey stands. This is believed to be the origin of the expression 'on the mat'.

The concern of this book is the protection of the horse and it was the Jockey Club Disciplinary Committee's job to ensure not only that the rules and instructions of racing were strictly followed for the benefit of all involved, but also that the wellbeing of the horse was paramount. It therefore came as a surprise when I was asked to chair what the *Times* headlined as this 'Top Jockey Club post' after just five years as a member. Once again I have no doubt that it was largely my career as a lawyer which propelled me into the job. The *Times* correspondent, Richard Evans, drew the same conclusion, saying of me on 6 October 1995 that my appointment would be 'a lightning promotion within the Jockey Club. However, his legal background is considered invaluable in dealing with the policing and regulation of racing at a time when other sports' governing bodies are facing increasing challenges to their powers in the courts.' Racing was certainly becoming increasingly litigious. There was a time when jockeys attended disciplinary meetings alone, while today they are often accompanied by their lawyer, and the committee itself might have legal representation. It all just adds to the cost.

I was succeeding an exceptional chairman of the committee, Anthony Mildmay-White, who had introduced some wide-ranging changes, but still the arguments about the whip and other disciplinary matters refused to go away. Anthony had appointed as full time Director of Regulations Malcolm Wallace, whom I knew well before I started, and this enabled us to make good progress. I knew I was going to be busy and I chose retirement from my 'day job' as a solicitor in mid-1996 to clear the decks for what lay ahead.

The role of the Jockey Club has now changed and it seems appropriate to end this chapter with the words of Nicholas Wrigley, who retired as Senior Steward in June 2014:

'There was naturally a nervousness that the Jockey Club's power and influence would disappear when we lost our regulatory powers, but we have a different form of power now. Our strong commercial position, allied with the whole ethos of the Jockey Club as a force for good in racing, gives us huge authority. We are not doing it for our own commercial interest, so people listen.' (Malcolm Armytage, *Daily Telegraph*, 5 June 2014).

Early rescue transport

Four rescues from the past – but neglect continues today

Ada Cole, founder of ILPH

Early international transport

Left: The terror felt by this horse can only be imagined

Above: Only a small improvement from a crane

Below: Antwerp Dockside – The sort of sight that inspired Ada Cole

Above: The effect of ill-fitting harness, Honduras

Below: WHW farriery course in Choluteca, Honduras

Winning hearts and minds – teaching through theatre, Honduras

A basic cart, heavily laden – a common sight in Honduras

*Digger and young 'handler',
Belwade Farm*

Digger on parade with Household Cavalry

Ian Kelly, former Director of International Training

The 'Dallas-style' round up of feral ponies in Scotland with Horseback UK

Farriery class, Senegal

Emma Swadlo, field officer, winning trust on Erith Marshes, Kent

David Boyd, chief field officer, and rescues

Sarah Tucker, field officer, and rescue

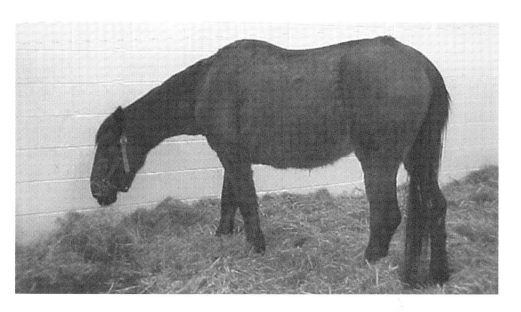

Before – Penny on arrival at Penny Farm

After – Penny recovered serving with King's Troop

Penny with Penny Thornton, founder of Penny Farm!

Eight neglected thoroughbreds arrive at Glenda Spooner Farm

Learning to be loved again, Penny Farm

Pony assessment at Hall Farm

Saddlery course, Guatemala

WHW supporting the Soweto Equestrian Centre

WHW national call centre, Hall Farm

Author "in training"

5 | THE DISCIPLINARY COMMITTEE

On 1 July 1996 I became chairman of the Jockey Club Disciplinary Committee and one of the seven stewards of the Club, and walked straight into the flak flying around the subject of whip abuse. This argument would take a good deal of my time and, to this day, continues to be a running sore in racing's story. After so many years' debate, we seem unable to agree if hitting a horse is cruel, if it simply encourages an animal or if it should be banned altogether.

My predecessor, Anthony Mildmay-White, had approached me at Cheltenham in March 1995 and asked if I would be prepared to take on the job. I was surprised, as I was still a relative newcomer to the Club, but I suppose that the other stewards had considered me to have performed adequately on such things as the Harness Racing Proposal. The whip was the dominant issue and I presume they thought a legal mind was again required.

It wasn't long before there was uproar in the racing world when, in September, Frankie Dettori and Pat Eddery, having ridden what everyone agreed was one of the most thrilling finishes to the Pertemps St Leger at Doncaster, were both suspended for overuse of the whip. Dettori rode the winner, Shantou, and Eddery was on Dushyantor. This was precisely the sort of race that the punters come to see, but the jockeys fell foul of the new rules and, according to those rules, Dettori had not given his horse time to respond between hits and had used unreasonable force, while Eddery had used his whip too often.

The press were all over the story, demanding changes to the rules which they thought were too rigid. Others called for an outright ban on whips. The consensus was that while rules had to be obeyed and those who broke them punished, there had to be some flexibility within them.

The row brought out every view: there was the 'horses are stupid' brigade who believed they need to be driven on, the 'horses are bred for a purpose' school of thought, for whom racing under a whip is part of a horse's job, and the 'never again' contingent, who were in favour of a ban. Racehorses are bred for a purpose, but that is no excuse, even when the prize is great, to beat a horse which is already straining every sinew to win. Sheikh Mohammed told the *Racing Post* at the time: 'My honest opinion is that if a horse was fifth on heavy ground, then you can't really have a go at him. But this is a Classic and what do you want to do? You will have no racing otherwise. I understand the rule about hitting the horse when you have no chance, but when you are fighting for a Classic sometimes you don't think about that.'

Patrick Hibbert-Foy, the Senior Steward's secretary on duty on the day, was quite certain what he had witnessed and said so: 'It was sad that we had to take action because it was a brilliant ride, but it was outside the guidelines laid down by the Jockey Club. Dettori hit Shantou 13 times and never allowed his horse time to respond to the whip before using it again. He was hitting Shantou on virtually every stride and, although Dettori does sometimes flick the whip, he wasn't flicking it on Shantou – he really meant it.' (*Sporting Life*, 16 September 1996). And this was perfectly clear when I, together with Malcolm Wallace and Patrick, reviewed the film of the St Leger afterwards.

What were the stewards to do? Just because there might be thousands of racegoers or even hundreds of thousands of pounds at stake, should they somehow turn a blind eye to breaches of the rules when they occurred on the big occasions? Malcolm summed matters up in this way: 'If a rule is in place, it is exercised throughout racing and there is absolutely no chance of it being relaxed for the major races.'

The rule in question in 1996, H9, gives examples of improper use of the whip, which some may regard as self-evident:

1. Hitting horses which are: out of contention; showing no response; clearly winning; past the winning post.

2. Hitting horses: with the whip above shoulder height; out of their stride pattern; to the extent of causing injury.

3. Hitting horses in any place except: on the quarters with the whip in either the backhand or forehand position; down the shoulder with the whip in the backhand position; unless very exceptional circumstances prevail.

4. Hitting or appearing to hit horses with unreasonable force or frequency.

We undoubtedly felt under pressure because the focus had shifted from the splendour of the occasion onto an argument over a breach of rules and the suspension of two of the best jockeys in the game, who were riding, let us not forget, two outstanding horses. Jockeys like the flamboyant Dettori are crowd pullers and the last thing any steward wants to do is detract from the enjoyment of top-class racing.

There was, on the other hand, no question of ducking the issue and we were always going to stick by the letter of the law regardless of any bad publicity; having said that, I noted in my own diary at the time that once again the rules would have to be revised. Anthony Mildmay-White, despite his best efforts by introducing his innovative 'totting up' process to punish repeat offenders on the racecourse, had nonetheless left me with a problem.

The suspensions stood but my concern, as always, despite all the negative publicity, was for the wellbeing of the horse. Simply counting how many times a jockey had hit a horse, even in the heat of the final furlong, was not good enough and so we stopped that rigid analysis. My committee and I said the stewards must first ask themselves: 'Did it cause you concern?' If it did, then they had to look at the film again and consider how much force had been used and whether or not it was effective, did the horse have time to respond and where was it being struck, on the quarter or in the stifle? I wanted stewards to look and listen to all the evidence before them in order to reach an appropriate verdict and not be caught in a straitjacket. The BHA in their turn have also addressed the problem and ultimately come back to the conclusion that stewards must be allowed an element of discretion in their decision making.

Sometimes the evidence at a stewards' enquiry would be clear cut: yes, a horse cut in front of another and caused interference which affected the result of the race, and a placing might have to be reversed. Those sorts of decisions had to be swift because the bookmakers and the punters were waiting with their betting slips in their hands. But issues of excessive use of the whip where the outcome of a result would not be affected might, and usually did, take much longer.

The six-hit rule was itself an amendment introduced in 1993 to the ten-strike limit, but eventually we agreed in November 1996 to abandon the six-hit rule and apply what we considered to be a more common sense approach, amounting to 'Did the riding cause offence?' Some might favour the advice of the late Harry 'Tom' Jones, horse trainer from 1951 to 1996, which he gave in a seminar to stewards: 'In the absence of total disaster, for God's sake leave the result alone.' I only wish that it were always so straightforward.

On the whole, the veterinary profession agrees that careful use of the whip is not harmful to horses and that is what was - and remains - my primary concern. In racing the whips are 68 cm long, including the flap at the end, and a minimum of 1 cm in diameter. There is a template on the desk of the Clerk of Scales in the jockeys' weighing room which is used to measure the length of their whips. All jockeys' whips now have a felt cover tip and are softer as a result.

When stewards are trying to decide if a horse has been unreasonably hit, they can simply pick up their radios and ask the on-duty vet for their opinion. It is the vet's responsibility to inspect the horse as soon as possible after the race and see if there are any weal marks. This is a fairly rare occurrence but some horses are known to mark very easily and even after the St Leger row, both horses were reported the following day to be in exuberant form and none the worse for wear.

The arguments and the agonies of controversial rulings were always, and still are, vociferously played out in the press. On one occasion, Peter Cundell, then President of the National Trainers' Federation, accused the Jockey Club, along with William Nunneley, a stewards' secretary, and Malcolm Wallace in particular, of victimising Richard Guest when he and trainer Kate Milligan were penalised for excessive use of the whip at Perth in May 1998. Cundell told *The Sporting Life*: 'It is a blatant travesty of justice.' Feelings run high in this passionate sport.

After another thrilling finish, this time in the Juddmonte at York in August 1998, Pat Eddery, Frankie Dettori and Kieren Fallon received eight-, four- and three-day bans respectively for excessive use of the whip. Alastair Down, writing in the *Racing Post*, stated: 'Racing involves a degree of cruelty and we have a set of rules in place to ensure that the level of cruelty is kept within the bounds of the acceptable.' He argued that racing would be the poorer without the whip. Are there really 'bounds' within which cruelty is acceptable?

If I thought racing were cruel I, for one, would not be involved and I do not apologise for repeating that, to me, the horse always comes first. But who will speak up for the horse? In part of a presentation made by the Jockey Club to the Parliamentary All Party Racing Committee on 13 April 1999, Dr Peter Webbon, our Chief Veterinary Adviser, opened his remarks on the Safety and Welfare of Horses by saying that the Veterinary Department 'acts as the voice of the horse', a wonderful phrase from a man who incidentally was awarded his doctorate for his study on tendon problems in horses. He went on to become Chief Executive of the Animal Health Trust which conducts important research work at its base just outside Newmarket.

There is still no conclusion to the whip debate, which was a hot topic even in the 1980s, to judge by cuttings of mine dating back to that time. There is consensus, though, that there have to be rules and punishments to protect the horses. Ideas have ranged from banning the horse as well as the rider, which seems harsh on the horse, to heavy fines including loss of prize money, which also cause negative publicity. At Ascot in 2013, a French rider initially lost his winning jockey percentage of the prize fund – about £50,000 – because he had hit his horse too many times. This ruling was subsequently revoked following an outcry in the racing press and elsewhere.

The Jockey Club considered the arguments long and hard before changing any rules, and we also had considerable experience upon which we could draw. Wise voices such as that of David Oldrey, who served as a steward for eight and a half years and was said to have the most analytical brain in racing, were always ready to offer advice, not for reasons of self- aggrandisement but for the benefit of racing and the horse. I recall him quietly asking me, when we were considering some rule change, if we had thought about a particular issue or considered some other aspect which, from his long experience, he thought might help our deliberations. I would echo comments that he was a shy genius; he is a racing man to his core and a person of great tact.

Another hugely experienced man is Christopher Foster, the Chief Executive of the Club, who was initially employed by Weatherbys in 1973. He is formally known as the Keeper of the Match Book, a hand-written record of every race run at Newmarket between 1 October 1718 and 11 November 1788. He has a sharp mind and good sense of humour and always sits at the right hand of the Senior Steward at the monthly meetings of the Jockey Club stewards. He always took a keen interest in disciplinary matters and, while I would not always agree with him, I appreciated his long experience and his connections in horse racing which are world-wide. There were certainly occasions when he made me think again.

There is no fool-proof answer but solutions can and will be found in education; some apprentice races now have riders only permitted to use 'hands and heels' to drive their mounts forward, which was a project initiated by Malcolm to develop essential skills without too much reliance on props. At the strictly amateur ordinary-rider level, I carry a stick for correction and safety. The public needs to understand exactly what is happening in those flashing, final moments in a race. Is the jockey hitting the horse or simply waving his whip and, if he is hitting, why is he doing it and what effect is it having?

Even champion jockeys need a reminder on occasion. AP McCoy had to undergo formal tuition at the jockeys' Racing School in Newmarket after being found to be repeatedly in breach of the rules, which was not quite as he suggested in his second autobiography. He didn't choose to go back to the racing school 'to try to figure it (the use of the whip) out' – he was sent back, muttering angrily to the *Racing Post* in the lead-up to his punishment: 'I feel like giving the whole game up and going off and playing golf. I've been done so many times for excessive force it's just a joke.' He also claimed in his book that I was on site at the training school to watch proceedings, with the suggestion, I suppose, that I was there to gloat at his 'humiliation'. I was not, in fact, there. He now acknowledges that small blip in his recollection and conceded in the earlier version of his autobiography that we had done him a service. He finally realised that we were serious, having made him sit down with us at Portman Square to study film of his technique, along with 15-times champion trainer, Martin Pipe, and his wife Carole.

Martin had stated to the press that he did not understand the rules, despite confirming in his trainer's licence application that he did! I wrote to him, suggesting that as he had signed that form, he should visit us in London to discuss the rules. When he and Carole arrived, I noticed that his wife had brought a foolscap sheet of written questions to ask. Since I had convened the meeting, I said that I would speak first and showed them the films in which it was all too clear that AP McCoy was not hitting the horses on the quarter but quite frequently on the stifle, which was not allowed. Silence reigned. When I asked Carole Pipe if she would like to say something, her list was abandoned. 'Nothing,' she said. We did not laugh at the time but I have teased her regularly since.

In my personal notes of the occasion, I wrote that AP had to change his style of riding and that, if he were Tim Henman, his tennis coach would be analysing his every shot. Pipe got his own back when I visited his yard in October 2013. He put me up on his mechanical horse to see how I got on. I refused to use a whip.

McCoy, who became the BBC's Sports Personality of the Year in 2010, told me once, possibly in jest, that his favourite Cheltenham ride had been a horse called Hors de la Loi. He will always be considered one of the great jockeys and is certainly well aware when he is stepping 'outside the law'. Maybe he simply accepts so many rides that from time to time he is bound to find himself before the stewards; having had an unblemished run since 2012, he received another ban after Aintree in 2014. I doubt, though, that anyone will ever match his remarkable career. In 2015 he announced his retirement at the top of his game when he became champion jump jockey for the twentieth successive year. He is made of tough stuff, having broken nearly every bone in his body from his cheekbones to his ankles. He is simply indestructible. I admire him very much.

One of the messages which came across loud and clear was to ensure consistency in rulings by the stewards at the 59 racecourses round the country. While the Jockey Club did not want to be continually over-ruling local decisions, it was important that uniformity of standards was applied and, to this end, we regularly travelled round the country holding seminars for stewards, ensuring that they were crystal clear about the rules. Occasionally, one steward seemed to dominate a group of stewards at a racecourse and some gentle persuasion was required to remind them that there could only be one interpretation of the rules: the Jockey Club rule book.

Another point, which was not generally realised, was that stewards were appointed for one year only and that their 'performance' was reviewed annually. Because most stewards were reconfirmed in their posts it was usually, but erroneously, assumed that it was a post until the age of 70 and I suspect that many stewards themselves were blissfully unaware that reports and notes by racecourse executives and other sources were reviewed every year.

All new stewards had to attend a training course and not everyone was accepted, which was quite a snub, particularly as these people were volunteering for an unpaid job; in the early days stewards did not even get a mileage allowance. Existing stewards, regarding the job as a privilege, had to attend one of 12 training seminars we ran every year to ensure that everyone was up to speed with new regulations. There were additional courses for those seeking promotion to Chairman to ensure that they were capable of chairing an enquiry, the most important of which are now under the all-seeing eye of the TV camera. Not everybody passed the test. Stewards' secretaries were also given training days every quarter, as we did all we could to keep decision making as uniform as possible. We endeavoured, in other words, to make sure that everyone involved in an official capacity was properly prepared and adhered to the basic principles, even if the quality of stewarding was variable. I attended these training days with Malcolm Wallace and on one occasion there was a lengthy discussion about how the interference rules should be interpreted. Eventually, one of the stewards, Paul Barton, said: 'What does Christopher think?' Having committed myself, Paul then commented: 'Well that is that, then.' Even now, I am not at all sure that he agreed with me. Malcolm believed that the only answer to this problem was stewarding by professionals. I still disagree, and although his view might eventually win the day, that in itself will not prevent argument and criticism.

On the whole these seminars were well received, although on one visit to Lambourn, when we went to speak to trainers about the 151 rule on non-triers, we were concerned about the reception that we thought might await us. In the event, it went well, but Malcolm, half-jokingly, still suggested that I should check my car in case a bomb had been put under it. I did, of course.

Being a steward does occasionally carry some risk. Over the years my family has run many different horses in point-to-point and hunter chases. Nadjati and all our subsequent horses have been discovered for us by our agent, David Smyly. At the mention of David's name at a dinner once, my neighbour asked: 'Surely you know the story about him?' It transpired that David was a Jockey Club judge. He was judging at Pontefract in Yorkshire, at the time a mining and heavy industry area. The result of the race, a close finish, displeased the race goers so much that - legend has it - they burnt the Judge's box to the ground. It wasn't quite so dramatic when Malcolm and I went to Catterick to talk to local trainers about the rules, as we had done at Lambourn. One of the horses in the yard of the well-known trainer Mary Reveley was found not to be trying. Mary was in tears as we tried in vain to explain the decision. Harvey Smith, whom I knew well from his show jumping career but who was only assistant trainer to his wife, Sue, leapt to her defence, as I think he thought we were bullying Mary. Harvey was not someone to be messed with and I felt something close to fear!

There is no logical argument against Rule 151. How can anyone justify entering a horse for a race when they know it has no chance of winning? It is dishonest to the punters. There is no question that the practice has gone on for years but today, with TV cameras and high quality images, compared with the grainy footage of old and a steward's opinion based on a fleeting view through his binoculars, there can be no denying the evidence.

When the arguments were flying in the press, particularly after controversial rulings, the Jockey Club was variously accused of burying its head in the sand or somehow of living in its Portman Square ivory tower, guided by 'incompetent stewards' on the racecourse. That could not have been further from the truth. While I was chairman of the Disciplinary Committee, we made it a priority to know every single steward in the country and for them to know us.

Jockeys, trainers and stables all have to be licensed and it was not only jockeys who could, in the worst cases, lose their licence. We had inspectors who visited stables to ensure that the highest standards of horse welfare and security were being maintained. In a smaller yard, the stables may not be properly managed or the horses may look run down. We had the power, which still exists, to send our vets to carry out an inspection without notice and, if they were concerned, the trainers were given, say, three months to sort matters out under pain of losing their training agreement.

It was also our job to help when trainers fell out with owners, perhaps when they failed to pay training fees. One trainer complained to us that his foreign-based owner owed a very considerable sum but had failed to pay up. I asked if he had a standard trainer's agreement and, sadly, he had not. He had felt that it was unnecessary as the owner was well known and he was carried away with the vision of a big, high-spending owner. There was little we could do and I advised him to try his luck in the courts.

Nor were we afraid to speak out when we thought we saw foul play in other quarters of racing. Rumour and gossip have always bubbled under the surface about cheating, race fixing and even money laundering, and I have no doubt that will continue. In October 1999, when Christopher Spence was Senior Steward, he gave a hard-hitting speech at the Gimcrack dinner in York. Addressing the bookmakers in particular, he said: 'Their business equally depends on the punters' trust in the integrity of racing. And yet when 'foul' or 'fix' is cried, for whatever reason, and often by the larger firms, we, surprisingly, receive no information about the people who struck bets with them, on the grounds of client confidentiality, when the information that they have may very well be the key to the perpetrator or perpetrators being brought to justice. This is evidence of the need for greater regulation of the betting industry and in particular for disclosure of information.'

The response was a challenge from the bookmakers to put up or shut up. Chief Executive of William Hill, John Brown, said: 'If the Jockey Club asks for information, we give them as much help as we legally can, but we stop short of naming names.' (*Racing Post*, 9 December 1999).

The lowest point for any group of stewards must be to call off racing for the day and during my time as chairman of the Disciplinary Committee that low point was without doubt reached at the infamous second October meeting at Haydock Park in 1996. It was a bad day for racing and many lessons were learned, but at the heart of it were two key points: the rules had to be followed by stewards as well as by jockeys and the safety of all concerned - riders and horses - was paramount.

Overnight rain had left the going heavy on 15 October. The first race went ahead despite concerns about the ground raised by jockeys at the start. After the race, a deputation of jockeys, led by Frankie Dettori, together with trainer Peter Chapple-Hyam, spoke to the stewards. A further inspection of the course was made and the stewards decided that the second race, the Sycamore Nursery, should go ahead and a public announcement was made. But the jockeys refused to go out and racing had to be abandoned for the day.

We announced that there would be an enquiry by the Disciplinary Committee and as I said at the time: 'The important point I want to get across is that this is not a witch-hunt against the jockeys. We have to have an enquiry to sort out whether rules were broken and that is what we will be doing.'

Unfortunately, the correct procedures were not followed that afternoon; the jockeys should have been informed before the public announcement was made and there was confusion about the decision among the jockeys as to whether they had been called out to race or not. Dettori had already decided on the way back from the course inspection that he considered it too dangerous to race, both for himself and his horses, and told the Steward's Secretary of his decision when he came to inform the jockeys that racing would proceed.

Our enquiry found that there was considerable misunderstanding among the jockeys, some of whom were already in their racing silks and skull caps waiting to be called out. We decided that 'blame for the failure in communication lies with the senior jockeys present who should have made their willingness to ride clear to the Stewards' Secretary' and that the actions of the Stewards 'did not comply fully with regulations'.

The net unhappy result was that a day's racing was lost, the Stewards were reprimanded and told that extra training was required, Frankie Dettori was found to be in breach of racing rules, although no further action was taken against him, and the 20 other jockeys were cleared of staging a strike. Unsurprisingly, there were disgruntled stewards who wrote to me privately expressing their disappointment at being singled out, but someone has to be in charge and the people in charge at any race meeting are the stewards. The buck stops there. I took some comfort from a note sent to me by my former commanding officer, Monkey Blacker, also a former Chairman of the Disciplinary Committee, who assured me that, in his considerable experience, 'everything started at the top.'

The dilemma facing all concerned was neatly summed up in an article in *Horse Law* at the time: 'In debating an issue such as this it is very important to understand two things. The first is that it is the jockeys, not the officials or the punters, who are the ones who risk life and limb every time they get on a racehorse. Secondly, jockeys are probably (except for professional hunt servants) the toughest people in the equine world. If a top jockey says the track is dangerous, I believe him. Further bear in mind that if they do not ride, they lose money.' The article went on to raise the prospect of a rider being 'forced' to ride against his better judgement and then being injured in a fall – who would be to blame?

In some parts of the world, jockeys have no say. I recall watching camel racing in the Emirates where the riders could scarcely have been more than ten years old. The races were six kilometres, which were one circuit of the track, taking about eight minutes. The tiny boys were perched on top, 'glued' on with Velcro, it was rumoured – there were no fallers that day. There were signs everywhere saying 'No Photography', enforced by armed police, which I suspect had more to do with the possibility of the young jockeys being identified. One can only speculate why this should have been a concern.

Stewards are responsible for everything that happens, from the safety of horses and spectators to the efficiency of the medical facilities. On one occasion at Southwell, the doctors were found not to have the equipment required by the Jockey Club, and the racecourse was subsequently fined. Medical attention for jockeys has, without doubt, improved a great deal over the years. The same applies, in fact, to the entire conduct of a day's racing. If anything goes wrong, it always comes back to the stewards on duty. Perhaps that is why, in this age of hyper-sensitivity, the BHA has now banned stewards from having an alcoholic drink over lunch before the racing starts. I had discussed this with Lord Hartington when he was Senior Steward and he believed that there was nothing wrong with having a drink so long as people were fit to drive afterwards. He felt the same standards should apply. I adopted those rules whenever I was chairman of a panel of stewards and still think that to be a reasonable guideline. We are, after all, dealing with knowledgeable people with common sense.

The steward's lot is one full of reward and a matching degree of criticism. Imagine trying to find a happy balance when adjudicating in a possible case of interference where there might be a substantial difference in the pot between first and second place. I remember on one occasion the top trainer, Anne Herries, one of the daughters of the Duke of Norfolk, who had trained the winner of the Prix du Jockey Club at Chantilly in 1995, appealing against a ruling by the Ascot stewards to reverse the placings in a tight finish which put her horse Taufans Melody second. We upheld the ruling and afterwards, by way of conversation more than anything else, I said something about the huge disparity in prize money between the first (£53,000) and second (£17,000) places, to which Lady Herries replied icily: 'I certainly didn't do it for that!' and turned on her heel and left. Just a few days later I met her husband, Colin Cowdrey, at a livery dinner in London where he was guest speaker. I asked him if he was speaking to me. He said: 'Not really, but with all that prize money we had to have a go.' I discovered later that what was uppermost in their minds were the highly profitable races in Australia, where to be eligible each horse had to have already won a certain amount of prize money, something they later achieved when Taufan's Melody won the 1998 Caulfield Cup as a 66-1 outsider.

Stewards very quickly learn to take on the chin whatever life throws at them: the tears and the tantrums from trainers, their wives and their jockeys all variously blustering and protesting their innocence. One has to see the funny side. So what makes a good steward? I can do no better than quote the inestimable Tom Jones once more: '...the vital ingredient in the composition of a perfect steward is common sense, and it is as rare a commodity in the press room as it is in the stewards' room, never mind the hot box, never mind in the betting shop.'

The jockeys in the Crabbie's Grand National on 5 April 2014 thought common sense was lacking when 39 of the 40 riders (Brendan Powell never started) were ordered before the stewards for lining up six seconds early for the start. In the ensuing confusion of the first false start, assistant starter, Simon McNeill, a former jump jockey, was knocked down. Although he was uninjured, the stewards on the day reported that the riders had compromised the welfare of an official.

Barry Geraghty, in his At the Races website column, accused the stewards of being 'high-handed', failing to apply common sense and treating the riders like 'school kids'. This attitude was echoed by AP McCoy in his *Daily Telegraph* column headlined: 'Aintree stewards should have used common sense.'

In protest, the jockeys refused to appear before the stewards and, with shades of Haydock 1996, left the course without being given permission and facing a two-day suspension. No further action was taken against the jockeys for that 'mutiny', but for lining up before being called forward by the starter they had to face the BHA Disciplinary Panel which, in the event, let them all off with a caution in June, nearly three months after the race. It was judged to be a small victory for the jockeys, but why did it take so long to reach a verdict?

Beyond trying to improve the training of stewards, I also sought in my time on the Disciplinary Committee to bring about some sort of harmony within the rules of racing in Europe, getting together with representatives from France, Germany, Italy and Ireland. In France, for example, the rule is that if you as the ultimate winner or placed horse interfere with another horse which comes, say, fifth, you should be placed sixth, even if the other horse stood no chance of winning. That is very different from the UK. French steward's enquiries are also different, as I found when sitting with French stewards at Deauville. They are conducted in a typically Gallic fashion with plenty of repartee between jockeys and stewards. The British rule is that the placings can only be changed if the stewards consider that the interference improved the placing of the horse causing the interference. The only time a horse can be disqualified is if the interference is considered dangerous. I spoke about interference in races at the FEI's International Conference of Horseracing Authorities in France in October 1998, with representatives from Australia, America and Germany as well as many others from Rome to Rio and Bangkok to Belgrade. Our aim was to achieve some sort of consistency and I showed a film of a race to gauge whether the example amounted to carelessness or recklessness and what penalties we should impose in Britain.

If a rider is penalised by stewards in one country, the penalty is normally recognised – reciprocated – in another. These are still very live issues. In May 2014, Pat Cosgrave challenged the decision by the Dubai stewards to impose a four-month ban for allegations of 'team riding' when he was said to have moved his horse, Anaerobio, off the rail to allow its stablemate, Vercingetorix, through to victory at Meydan in March. Cosgrave appealed against the ruling to the BHA, who decided not to reciprocate the ban and cleared him to continue riding in Britain.

Usually the suspension of a jockey is reciprocated internationally, although when Martin Dwyer was suspended for eight months by the Royal Western India Turf Club for preventing his horse, Ice Age, from running on its merits at the Mahalaxmi racecourse in Mumbai on 17 February 2013, the BHA rejected the findings. Jamie Stier, the BHA's director of Raceday Operations and Regulation said: 'It was the BHA's view that there were a number of areas during the process which fell short of being demonstrably fair.' Although Dwyer was free to ride, he said he was unlikely to race in India again. The Professional Jockeys' Association (PJA) said its members should be 'very cautious' about taking jobs in India in the future. My wife and I, with members of the Jockey Club, visited Mumbai for the 2014 Indian Derby. We were invited to join the Indian Stewards to watch the racing, but I did not raise the recent problems between us.

If nothing else, I hope I always applied common sense during my stint as Chairman of the Disciplinary Committee and that, by the time I stood down, I had left racing a marginally safer place for jockey and horse. Monkey Blacker kindly summed up my chairmanship as 'progressive', which is all one can hope for. To get the best out of a horse requires both knowledge and common sense; if an owner neglects their horse it will ultimately fail them, either through bad temper or, worse, through ill health. The rules of racing are there not to punish or penalise but to ensure fairness and the safety of all involved, and it has always been my concern to champion the one element that cannot defend itself – the horse. Before I left my official duties in racing to focus more on the welfare of horses, I had one more task to perform for horse racing.

6 | THE APPEAL BOARD

would like to say that the horse racing world was beginning to get the message that no infringement of the rules would escape detection and punishment but, far from slowing up, the number of cases coming before the Disciplinary Committee showed no sign of abating as my stint as Chairman came to an end in 2000. Its replacement body at the BHA, called the Disciplinary Panel, still seems to have its hands full as a cursory glance at the equestrian pages reveal: the whip debate, of course, continues but, sadly, so does the more sinister practice of doping.

In 2000, the Jockey Club still had some work for me to do when it launched a new Appeal Board, in large part to satisfy the demands of the Human Rights Act. In December, I was invited to join the panel of Board members, which was in effect the last stop in the 'legal' process for those seeking redress from a ruling by stewards or the Disciplinary Committee itself. (The only difference since 3 November 2014 is that the BHA itself can appeal a ruling by the Disciplinary Panel.) The Appeal Board was drawn from a panel of half a dozen Jockey Club members; for each hearing three of us would be selected to sit with a barrister.

Under the normal process, if the winner or any other horse in a race failed a drugs test, it would be referred to the Disciplinary Committee and the trainer or owner involved, if the ruling went against them, could then take it to the Appeal Board. Initially the 'appellant' usually came alone, although increasingly they would have legal representation, and generally our decision was accepted. We would meet three or four times a year, so it was much more leisurely than the almost daily challenges that were thrown up by the Disciplinary Committee. (I remained a panel member of the Appeal Board for eleven years.)

The grounds for an appeal ranged from straightforward disagreement with the Disciplinary Committee's decision to a claim that the hearing had been unfair or prejudicial, that there was a lack of evidence, that the Rules of Racing had not been properly applied or that the penalty imposed was disproportionate. The actual proceedings were then fairly standard: written statements were taken, oral submission could be made and, subject to certain guidelines, any new 'evidence' could also be presented on the day of the hearing. This all makes it sound very much like a legal process, which I suppose, in a way, it was, with reputations at stake along with the potential value of the horse at stud.

When I say that the Appeal Board's decision was generally accepted, there was a landmark case in the summer of 2004 when the Irish trainer, Willie Mullins, rejected the findings of the Disciplinary Committee and the subsequent Appeal Board ruling. Sir Edward Cazalet, Anthony Mildway-White and I were hearing the case. We agreed with the Disciplinary Committee's decision which was that Mullins, albeit unwittingly, had been in breach of the rules because his horse, Be My Royal, had tested positive for morphine in its urine having won the Hennessey Cognac Gold Cup at Newbury on 30 November 2002. It transpired that the morphine was present in some batches of the popular horse feed Connolly's Red Mills 14% Racehorse Cubes, originating in the poppy seeds in the raw material used to manufacture the feed. No one in the Mullins yard could possibly have known about the contaminant but technically he was in breach, the horse was disqualified and £5,000 costs were awarded against him.

Mullins decided to test the ruling in the Queen's Bench Division of the High Court in October 2005. It was an important case for the Jockey Club and its independence. In the event, Mr Justice Stanley Burnton ruled that decisions of the Appeal Board were a matter of private and not public law and therefore, in the legal jargon, were not amenable to judicial review. He stated that the trainer and the Jockey Club had a contract which incorporated the rules of racing and despite the fact that there was an appeal board, it remained a private function rather than a public one. Citing the Aga Khan case in 1993, Justice Burnton made it clear that 'a private body could not by itself create a public body or convert a private function into a public function by creating an appeal board.' The case was thrown out and established once and for all that the Appeal Board had the final say and that there was no higher authority. This was an important ruling.

The danger of something being too private is that decisions can be construed as being unfair when not subject to public scrutiny, another pressure resulting from the Human Rights Act. I was always concerned that every decision we made should be perfectly transparent and, just as important, perfectly understandable; the policy of holding training seminars for stewards and stewards' secretaries was part of the same strategy.

Contaminated feed remains a problem to this day and no one is immune. The Queen's horse, Estimate, runner up in the 2014 Ascot Gold Cup, tested positive for morphine. The quantity was microscopic and all seemed to agree that it would have had no effect on the horse's performance, but the BHA has a zero-tolerance approach to morphine on race days - it is only allowed in training as a pain killer or a sedative. Again the culprit was an ingredient supplied to the feed manufacturers, Dodson and Horrell. Rogue poppy seeds getting into crops used for the feed, alfalfa chaff, appear to have been the cause. No blame was attached to the trainer, Sir Michael Stoute, but Estimate was disqualified and the Queen forfeited her £80,625 prize money. A second Stoute-trained horse and six others also tested positive. Such contamination is difficult to spot. Clare Williams of the British Equestrian Trade Association said: 'We might be talking about a dozen poppy seeds in a two tonne batch of food. It's like looking for a needle in a haystack and the pocketed nature of the contamination is such that it can be difficult to find the hot spots despite rigorous controls.'(*Daily Telegraph*, 24 July 2014)

Meanwhile, in the summer of 2002, I was asked to chair a committee looking into the possibility of opening up the Portman Square and racecourse stewards' enquiries to the press, given that the perception in some quarters was that the stewards were acting as judge, jury and prosecution. Today, opening proceedings to the public may seem perfectly sensible, yet while the general consensus at that time was in favour of the move, there were concerns. Some feared that if televised enquiries were introduced at racecourses, jockeys and stewards might either be inhibited by the cameras, if not natural 'performers' or, worse, might be tempted to grandstand.

Michael Caulfield, executive manager of the Jockeys' Association of Great Britain at the time, cautioned: 'It might make good TV, but our members' experience from being involved in different parts of the world is that people tend to act in front of an audience. Jockeys are not trained advocates, nor should they be expected to be.' (*Daily Telegraph*, 24 December 2002).

The only real difficulty facing enquiries at Portman Square was a matter of the space required to accommodate the press who might want to attend; they didn't care for our initial suggestion of just one representative from the Press Association and one from the trade press. The reality, of course, was that only the high-profile cases would attract much attention and, when they occurred, we could be sure the press gallery would be full.

At the time, television was looking critically at racing, the cheating and the doping scandals, and we had to show ourselves to be beyond reproach. Perhaps surprisingly, the flat jockeys were initially not in favour, whereas today every rider has to be something of a TV celebrity, with microphones thrust into their faces before they have even dismounted at the end of a race; instant assessments of the ride are demanded and predictions of future form are sought. It is to their credit that they all seem to play their new role well. Some, understandably, feel that their first obligation is to the owner and trainer before the media.

The fact that we were even debating the issue of public access probably seemed very old fashioned in parts of the world such as Australia, where racing enquiries had been open to the media for 40 years, and the process seemed to drag on for an inordinately long time. Finally, in October 2002, after a couple of centuries of conducting our business behind closed doors, the first Portman Square enquiries began to be open to the press, but it would take a while before the TV cameras finally pushed their way into racecourse stewards' enquiries.

And what of the fear that the presence of TV would make the whole process a bit of a show, degrading the enquiry to just part of the entertainment? John Maxse, the Jockey Club's public relations director, said at the time: 'As regulator, our motive for opening up enquiries is to increase the accountability and transparency of the decision-making process rather than for entertainment purposes. The opening up of disciplinary panel enquiries would be a big step for the sport. Indeed, we are not aware of any other comparable tribunals which allow a press presence at hearings.'

So much has changed for the better since I first became involved in racing, when I accepted the invitation to become a steward at Plumpton. It was this increasing push towards more openness, an effort to keep the public informed at race meetings, which has made one of the biggest differences. It was no longer good enough to announce a stewards' enquiry and subsequently that placings had been reversed. The announcement had to say more, give details, perhaps, of interference or whatever formed the basis for the stewards' decision. In short, with critics constantly circling looking for the slightest whiff of malpractice, everything had to be above board.

One of the proponents of such transparency was the late Sir Stan Clarke, Jockey Club member, property developer and, later, philanthropist who raised huge sums for Lichfield Cathedral. He had embraced racing with gusto, owning many winners, including the 1997 Grand National winner, Lord Gyllene. He went on to buy up racecourses including Brighton, Fontwell Park, Yarmouth, Uttoxeter, Bath, Hereford, Chepstow, Sedgefield and Newcastle, injecting new life into them. Above all, he believed in keeping in touch with his work customers and he adopted the same approach at his racecourses, even placing signs in his cloakrooms asking: 'How are we doing?' and insisting that anyone with a complaint should report directly to him.

Plumpton, Folkestone and Fontwell were racecourses at which I was fortunate to become a steward; others included Goodwood, Ascot, and Sandown. Quite rightly, I had to attend the seminars I had led in order to be taught the latest rules by my successors.

If I have one criticism of racing in the UK, it is that there is too much of it. We have all-weather tracks which trainers obviously like, because they can run their horses regardless of the weather and a win in front of the owners is always good news. I am not saying that there cannot be a good race just because the horses and trainers may not be of the very top flight; two horses fighting it out to the finishing line is just as thrilling for a prize of £2,000 as it is for half a million or more and, thanks to the likes of Stan Clarke and others, racecourses are taking more trouble to look after owners and trainers. But small fields are disappointing for the race goers and if the 'entertainment' is not there, the attendances will continue to slide and some racecourses might disappear or lose their major sponsors.

I have seen something similar happen in the wider equestrian world in my capacity as legal adviser to the British Equestrian Federation which looks after the international side of equestrianism in different categories. This work involved talking to all the other bodies from the British Horse Society, the Pony Club, the world of dressage and all the different countries involved in the FEI. So many of these disciplines have now become fragmented and they are beginning to compete with one another for the public's attention and money. There are numerous welfare groups, riding clubs and associations and racing bodies which may be weaker as a result of their numbers and diversity.

For a time I was chairman of the Arabian Racing Organisation, which has one big day in August every year at Newbury, well supported by the Maktoum family; they also race at Hereford and elsewhere, and the sport is strong in France, where they have a more favourable betting regime. During my time we tried to expand the interest and stage more racing days at other racecourses, but essentially it remains a specialist area and, apart from its devotees, struggles to expand. Then there is the Arab Horse Society which is also finding it hard to attract a decent racing crowd and is probably trying to put on too many races with too few runners and scant prize money in the minor races.

While the rewards at the top for owners and trainers may be high in Flat and National Hunt racing, the standard fare for jockeys is modest. A flat jockey may get £100 per ride, while a jump jockey will get £130 for the added risk involved. Few travel by helicopter from course to course like some of the super stars; for the majority, it means making their way home, frequently sharing the cost of transport after what might have been a bruising day with little to show for it. They provided entertainment for, it's hoped, a reasonable crowd but their names will already have been forgotten before the last race.

However, it was not entertainment which would now be consuming much of my time. I was about to turn my attention to the welfare of horses – not just top-flight thoroughbreds but everyday horses and ponies (and donkeys) which were suffering, and continue to suffer, neglect and abuse around the world. In many countries, horses are an essential tool of the trade and as far removed from the glitz and glamour of a race meeting as one could get. The charity I was about to join sought to persuade their owners to care for them in such a way that they could actually get more out of their animals by feeding them better, looking after their feet, making sure the harnesses fitted properly and that they were not loyally working away in pain. From the outset I knew that we could only achieve this by gentle persuasion, never by laying down the law. And, like every charity, I knew we would be competing for people's hard-earned money to support us; well over half our funds came from legacies and, just like Stan Clarke, I recognised that we would have to look after our supporters and take their opinions into account. If the horse world, including racing, was seen to be promoting an uncaring attitude towards horses, with too many fallers over the bigger Grand National fences at Aintree or wanton drug abuse, our benefactors would go elsewhere.

I was asked to review the disciplinary function of the Jockey Club back in 1993 and, re-reading my comments more than two decades later, I was relieved to see that they still made some sense: 'to be fair but robust; to arbitrate swiftly and competently; to make sure professionals and amateurs were all properly trained.' Regardless of the equestrian discipline, it must surely be right to dispense justice without delay precisely to be fair to all concerned. As I left riding in competition to the next generation (my sons, Colin who rides in cross-country team chases, and Philip, who is now the point-to-point rider in the family and much more successful than his father), I hoped to bring some of the same lessons I had learned to the wider world. We were not going to rule or punish those who mistreated their animals because in all probability it was through ignorance or, as they saw it, the need to earn a living. Just as we sought to educate stewards, trainers and jockeys, though, so too we would be educating those who depended on their horses for survival. While it was never an excuse to be ignorant of cross-contamination of feedstuffs or drugs in a yard of thoroughbreds, I did not think it an excuse even in developing nations to plead ignorance when a horse is clearly lame because its hooves are not cared for or its skin is rubbed raw from ill-fitting harnesses or the shafts of the cart it is pulling.

7 | ANOTHER WORLD

Consider the contrast between the finery on display at Royal Ascot and the Royal International Horse Show, and the brutality of tired, starving and thirsty horses, often with foals at foot, destined for export to the salami factories of Europe. This is a snapshot of life continuing today for so many horses; on the one hand an existence of cosseted comfort, on the other neglect and suffering before an inevitable and painful end.

Perhaps there was also a certain inevitability that, after all the years of enjoyment my hunters and the thoroughbreds and the show jumpers had given me, I would one day have to repay the debt. To my shame I would in the past have struggled to name even a few horse charities or say what exactly they did. There are at least 150 and the work of most of them had simply passed me by, despite my lifelong interest in horses. As a trustee for some time, I had of course been aware of Racing Welfare, which although bearing rather a confusing name, exists to support all the other workers in the racing fraternity apart from jockeys. Beyond caring as well as I could for the horses I owned, and doing my bit as a steward to ensure that professionals did not abuse their rides, I never gave much thought to those horses and ponies living out of the limelight, or indeed those which had reached the end of their useful lives.

I was for many years a member of the RSPCA but resigned when the charity took a militant line, about fox hunting in particular. I wonder from time to time whether as a campaigning group they are even entitled to charitable status. The public evidently agreed that the charity had lost focus as it was widely reported that there had been a drop of £7 million in donations, although the charity said that the fall was as a result of a decline of £5.7 million in legacies from wills and only a £1.3 million drop in public donations. Tim Bonner of Countryside Alliance, said: 'People across the board are unhappy at the direction it (RSPCA) has taken. We hope that it can accept this and refocus on its core work, which is vitally important.' (*Horse and Hound*, 10 July 2014). I wouldn't be at all surprised if the Charity Commission had begun to ask if prosecutions brought in relation to fox hunting were properly the work of a registered charity. It was widely reported that the RSPCA was criticised by the District Court Judge, Tim Pattinson, who was dealing with a case in which the Heythrop Hunt, based in Oxfordshire, were alleged to have broken the law. The hunt pleaded guilty to four charges of intentionally hunting a fox with dogs, and a former huntsman and retired hunt master also pleaded guilty to the same charge. The judge commented on the huge legal costs run up by the RSPCA in bringing the case – nearly £330,000 – which he described as 'quite staggering' (*Metro*, 17 December 2012).

It seems that the RSPCA will continue to investigate hunts but leave it to the police to prosecute or not if a hunt is thought to be in breach of the 2004 Hunting Act. Tony Blair, Prime Minister at the time, is recorded as saying that he regrets the Labour Party's pressure and introduction of this legislation. 'By the end of it (the legislation), I felt like the damn fox.'(*Daily Telegraph*, 1 September 2010).

On the other hand a number of our field officers are former RSPCA inspectors. While in many cases an RSPCA inspector more used to dealing with dogs and cats will contact our local field officers and ask for advice in respect of a horse, pony or donkey, the advantage of the RSPCA involvement is that the charity is empowered to bring a prosecution for cruelty, which other charities are not. In 2014, there was a suggestion that the RSPCA might lose its prosecuting powers. This would be a concern for animal welfare as the onus would then fall on an already hard pressed police force who, among all their other duties, might not see animal welfare as a priority.

I became a trustee of what was then known as the International League for the Protection of Horses (ILPH) in 2005 after Bunny Maitland-Carew had tapped me on the shoulder at one of Sir Peter O'Sullevan's magnificent charity fund raising lunches and suggested that I should consider taking over from him as chairman; he had been chairman for seven years and had greatly improved the finances of the charity as well as its standing in the horse world. I should add, for those too young to remember, that Sir Peter had been the BBC racing commentator for many years, his voice instantly recognisable to any racing enthusiast. His charity lunch usually makes in excess of £200,000, which is then distributed between a number of horse-related and other charities, including WHW.

The ILPH has a proud history dating back to 1927 when its founder, Ada Cole, was moved to establish it having seen exhausted horses on Antwerp docks waiting to be herded off for slaughter. Ada Cole was a tough realist who had worked as a nurse during World War One, had been captured by the Germans and was only spared the death sentence for helping Allied prisoners escape by the signing of the Armistice in 1918. She recognised that increased mechanisation would inevitably mean the end for the working horse but she was determined that that end should not be cruel and uncaring. She campaigned for a change in the law but died before her dream became reality with the introduction in 1937 of the Exportation of Horses Act, which prohibited the export of live animals for slaughter from Great Britain.

That was then, but today, with the collapse of the Soviet Union and the opening up of European borders, the trade in horses for meat has significantly increased. The Italians insist on animals being live when they arrive and horses and foals are crammed into lorries driven all the way from Romania to Italy, sometimes in mid-summer. The transportation rules are still not being enforced and the world is turning a blind eye to what is happening. Ada Cole, though, had an answer to our refusal to hear the horror stories that we are told: 'It is your duty to hear,' she would say, adding: 'It is because people do not want to hear that nothing is done. I am going to make people listen.'

In February 2005, I visited the charity's headquarters at Snetterton in Norfolk for the first time. It is a hugely impressive complex with quarantine areas, stabling, yards, an indoor school, paddocks and, most importantly, a hospitality area – winning the hearts and minds of the public is vital. This is an international charity and as far back as 1950, it began working in France, Italy, the Netherlands, Spain, Greece and South Africa. In 1985, once again with Peter O'Sullevan's encouragement, the first international training course was launched in Morocco. From the outset it was clear to me that the charity had a tremendous workload which required control and co-ordination, not only to manage the UK operation but also to oversee projects from Ireland to The Gambia, Fiji and beyond.

When I became chairman on 3 May 2006, I was certain what my role should be. I had to spread the word, in particular using my contacts in the show jumping, hunting and horse racing world and to help raise the profile by talking, as Ada Cole would have wished, to anyone who would listen and perhaps also to those who would rather not hear.

I felt we also had to do one other thing: change the name from the rather unwieldy International League for the Protection of Horses, a name not well-recognised outside small equestrian circles, to World Horse Welfare (WHW), which seemed rather neatly to sum up what the charity was about, working as we were on a global scale. This change was eventually made in 2008, although our hard-working President, the Princess Royal, admitted to me that for a while she still thought of it as the ILPH. That same year I was delighted when WHW became an associate member of the FEI after almost three decades as the Federation's welfare advisors. WHW had become involved with the FEI in order that they should know who we were and what we were about – taking the Ada Cole approach of speaking to anyone who would listen – and the FEI is one of most important international bodies in the equestrian sports world. They were always very welcoming and Princess Haya of Jordan, President of the FEI until 2014, is a great supporter and generous contributor.

The link with horses in sport through the FEI is important, while always keeping their welfare as the top priority. Roly Owers put it well at a conference: 'We are proud to play a role through the FEI, to ensure sport horses enjoy welfare standards among the highest in the world... however, the sport industry also understands that whenever we find bad practice, we will challenge them.'

The charity's values are summed up on its website (www.worldhorsewelfare.org)

Our vision:
World Horse Welfare's vision is a world where every horse is treated with respect, compassion and understanding.

Our mission:
Our mission is to work with horses, horse owners, communities, organisations and governments to help improve welfare standards and stamp out suffering in the UK and worldwide.

Not only does WHW have a wealth of expertise in its four British farms, but it also has field officers – on average about 16 of them – covering the whole of the UK. They have an enormous workload and face tremendous challenges, as well as not a little risk, as they go about their business.

The WHW ethos is that horses should be used not abused, with a strong emphasis on 'used' – rehoused, rehabilitated and re-used. We don't just give them a reassuring pat when they arrive, treat their injuries and turn them out in a field. We believe that if they really cannot be rehabilitated – either because their owners just can't cope or because they have come to us as 'prosecution cases', when the police ask us to hold them pending court decisions – and we have tried everything possible to give them a new life and a new purpose through our rehoming scheme, then they have to be put down. We don't hoard horses just for the sake of it, whereas other charities keep them grazing in fields. To me, that may be just as cruel, because some of these horses have received five-star luxury treatment over the years, maybe as good racehorses or as hunters, show jumpers or event horses. They lived off the fat of the land and it is no way of life to be turned out, with possibly a shed to allow them to escape the worst of the weather and, if anyone remembers, a bowl of food. I suspect the horses feel and look neglected. The line to euthanase unwanted horses and ponies is a tough, pragmatic one and, as Barry Johnson, WHW Chairman and equine vet, says, not one from which the charity shies away, because the alternative is neither kind to the horse nor practical for the charity.

WHW has no legal powers whatsoever and sometimes has to rely on field officers viewing horses from footpaths or neighbouring farm tracks; people will cover up a horse in poor condition with a rug and the field officers need to look underneath to see if there is a problem; the rug may not have been removed for a long time. Inevitably, reactions can be hostile but the field officers will always try to deal with the problem on site because it may simply be that the owner hasn't realised that the horse has lost condition or even that the horse is too fat. Whenever there is doubt, the field officers will try to establish as much information as possible about the horse, its location, the state it is in and who the owner is. They will always try and contact the owner because there may be a good reason why the horse is looking skinny, for example.

Surprisingly, perhaps, WHW finds that overweight horses and ponies are a much greater welfare concern now than they once were. It costs significantly more, takes longer and is far more difficult to rehabilitate an obese horse than an emaciated one. Assuming there are no underlying problems, it takes around three months to get an emaciated horse back to the correct weight but around nine months to do the same for a horse which is obese through overfeeding. 'Right Weight' is one of our long-standing campaigns aimed, for once, at well-intentioned and caring owners who think they are doing the best for their horse.

In most instances, the field officers will give advice where they can. Where they cannot resolve the situation, the horse or pony might need to be brought into one of the charity's centres, while sometimes an owner will accept that it is time to put the horse down, which WHW can arrange.

Typically, WHW tries to rehabilitate and rehome the horses it takes in within ten months of their arrival at our farms. When they come in, each one is assessed at the same time by a vet, a farrier and a physiotherapist. That sounds expensive but in the long run saves money, as all three can agree on a course of treatment which will speed up the recovery process. That, of course, is the ideal situation, when perhaps an owner has agreed to sign over the horse or pony to the charity. When they do that, a tough condition is attached: the former owner must agree to have no further contact with the horse; they must not attempt to find out where the horse has been rehomed and they are not allowed to visit the horse at any of our farms.

If the owner will not sign the horse over, then the RSPCA or trading standards get involved as well. In order for us to get the horse into our care at that point, it is known as a Section 9 case. Section 9 of the Animal Welfare Act (England and Wales) covers circumstances in which an animal is likely to suffer, while Section 4 refers to circumstances in which an animal is actually suffering.

Unfortunately, many horses come in as prosecution cases and until their case can be resolved, the charity may only administer basic care, although every horse that comes to our farms undergoes a period of quarantine, either isolated individually or in the group in which they were admitted. We cannot do any rehabilitation work apart from, perhaps, teaching the horse which may never have been handled to be led in hand. In prosecution cases, everything we do to a horse in our care has to be noted and filmed. They have to be weighed constantly and all the information recorded as evidence for the court cases. It is not uncommon for these cases to take a year or more to come to court, during which time the horses and ponies cannot be rehomed.

Not only do we believe that horses are to be used but we also do our very best to teach people that this is so. We run seminars and the field officers liaise where need be with other animal welfare charities, schools and the police.

To understand just what I had taken on, I decided to go out as soon as possible with the field officers to watch and to learn. On one occasion, we had been alerted by the police that a member of the public had noticed a group of about six horses, apparently abandoned under a viaduct on the M20 motorway. Our field officer in Kent, Clare, was accompanied by a member of the British Horse Society and two policemen. There was no grazing, the horses had no water and it was a very hot day; in short, they had been left to fend for themselves in the dust on a waste-strewn site. They had clearly not been handled very much, although Clare managed to catch two of them. I asked what was to happen next, and Clare said that there was no need to worry, because the owners would turn up very soon. Sure enough, moments later, they did, claiming that they were just about to move the horses to some new ground on another site. We said that, in that case, we would follow them, and took much delight in following the overweight and perspiring owners as they trudged a couple of miles up the hill to another field, which was only slightly better but where, at least, water was available. It was a temporary solution but at least, for a time, the horses were better off. We had done all we could. Clare kept a good eye on them after our visit.

This was a minor example of what happens on a daily basis for our field officers in the UK. The police were there because it is against the law to neglect animals and they were fly-grazing illegally; the presence of the law also provides some protection from behaviour that is often threatening, as some of these cases illustrate. Where there is ignorance, WHW tries to be fair in its judgement, but where there is abuse, it tries to act swiftly and be equally robust.

Increasingly, the charity is being asked to take in groups of horses rather than individual ones. Many of these horses are almost wild, and are certainly not used to being handled. In one case in Hampshire, the charity had to pick up 62 horses, most of which had never been handled and, as is typical in these situations, there were countless other creatures alongside them – Poitou donkeys, pigs, sheep, rhea and llamas, all living in indescribable filth.

Our farm in Scotland, Belwade near Aboyne, faced an exceptional challenge when ponies which had once been used for trekking had been allowed to run wild. There were more than 100 of them roaming some 2,000 acres of hill land; they were inter-breeding and all needed to be wormed, deloused or have their feet trimmed. There was inevitable infighting among the stallions and their welfare was paramount.

In order to round up and treat so many, WHW called in the help of Horseback UK, a charity which helps rehabilitate ex-servicemen, some of whom may have suffered amputations. They ride quarter-horses which respond to different aids. The former soldiers, along with fourteen Royal Marines, also had vital map reading and tracking skills which proved essential to cover the ground. After a recce of the terrain of steep hills, ravines and rivers, the teams managed to corral the ponies into holding pens so that they could all be treated and the colts and stallions castrated by surgeons and student vets from the Royal Dick School of Veterinary Studies in Edinburgh, to curb the breeding and allow the land they were living on to sustain the herds. It was a challenging but satisfactory operation undertaken over three days, which enabled 93 of the horses to be sold on later for brighter and more fulfilling lives. Scottish international event rider and three-times winner of Badminton Horse Trials, Ian Stark, took a great interest in this project and rehomed seven of the ponies. Some of them are still used every day in his riding school, teaching children to ride, and one, a cob, is used twice a week by Riding for the Disabled. In October 2014, the Princess Royal opened the Ian Stark Equestrian Centre near Selkirk.

As WHW is increasingly taking in multiple horses, we now have a system of pens and crushes in place in some of our farms to handle large groups of what are effectively wild horses when they are unloaded from lorries. This allows us to treat the ones which have been signed over to us, micro-chip them and inject them in safety.

In another instance, in Saxmundham in Suffolk, the charity was alerted to three ponies wandering near a railway line. When we tracked down the owner, we found dogs everywhere. Our field officer was suspicious when he noticed one other pony in a shed and asked if he could come back and look in the buildings. The owner refused so a warrant was issued and served by the police who went in first because the owner had a gun. They found 32 ponies and 50 dogs. The ponies were in every nook and cranny in barns and little pens. One pony stallion was in a pen surrounded by eight mares in season and he was going out of his mind. Eighteen of the ponies were stallions, very aggressive and emaciated. WHW worked until past midnight to collect up the ponies and get them back to Hall Farm.

The owner was asked why she kept so many ponies and she said it was because she loved them, which is a favourite statement; they cannot understand that animals being abused when stabled in this way are not happy. One field officer was told by a psychologist who worked in prisons that it was much like the mentality of paedophiles, who fail to realise the gravity of what they are doing and actually think children like what is happening to them. Horse hoarders are obsessive. At some point along the road they take a wrong turn, and that is when the problems begin. They live in squalor themselves and, thinking that the norm, assume that horses must like living in the same conditions. The field officer said that he could go blindfold into a house and realise at once that there is a problem.

Barry Johnson believes it is just too easy to set up a charity and explains how things can quickly go wrong: 'All the horse charities were set up by middle class, middle aged, well-meaning ladies, it doesn't matter whether it is the Brooke Hospital for Animals, The Donkey Sanctuary or WHW (ILPH), these ladies started them and were the driving force behind them. Indeed it was their force of character which enabled them to succeed. However, what tends to happen with the vast majority is that the founders get older and, when their health fades, there isn't a governance or financial structure to take the charity forward. The successful ones are where people have had the foresight to put in place such a structure but there are probably a thousand and one small charities which all claim to look after horses, and they do. They look after the first one very well, they look after the second one quite well and the third one not quite as well, and then they run out of money, so they take short cuts by not doing things, such as getting in the farrier and the vet, and then there is a welfare problem, and it can turn into a huge welfare problem, even though they set out with the best intentions to set up a horse rescue charity. But it nearly always ends in tears and then these good hearted people find themselves being prosecuted, which is certainly the last thing they thought of in the beginning when they set out to help horses.'

Ignorance or even a little knowledge is often the reason for much abuse and even the internet can be to blame. Jacko, one of the field officers, has a particular dislike of what he calls the feeding frenzy on Facebook. He was called by a member of the public to the worst case of mud fever he had ever seen. The horse was hobbling on three legs. The owner had been treating it with cream and wrapping the affected leg in cling film because that was what someone had recommended in the chat room; of course, the microbes were simply being kept warm and the situation had got worse. By the time the vet arrived the horse – a 4-year-old, 16-hand thoroughbred – had also developed colic and had to be put down.

On another occasion, a man had moved down from Liverpool to the Suffolk countryside. He had no knowledge of how to look after a horse but that had not stopped him going on to Gumtree to buy four ponies which he kept in three stables because 'his wife had always wanted a horse'. Some people see keeping a horse as a fashion statement, but buying a horse is the easy part. Having a horse is a status symbol with travellers so they will fight to keep one, even if it might have a broken leg, as was the case with one owner.

Someone else believed what they were told on the internet and went off to buy a full Hanoverian for £3,000, take it or leave it as seen. The horse was in a terrible state and when the previous owner was contacted, they said the horse had had a fractured pelvis and had been sent to the slaughter house. The slaughterman was selling the horses on instead of putting them down and the dealer was making a profit. This is just part of the dark underside of the horse world where money is the only motivation and welfare is never considered.

Perhaps what people are most familiar with is the sight of dozens of horses fly-grazing in the fields alongside motorways. Some counties are now so concerned after instances of fatal traffic accidents that they have taken drastic action. There are moves to introduce a protocol, as for stray dogs. The horses are picked up by bailiffs and, if no one claims them within 14 days, they are put down. Some private landowners have even been known to take the law into their own hands by using bailiffs – often tough ex-special servicemen, paratroopers and commandos – who are very effective and slick operators at dealing with stray horses. They are building up such a reputation that all they have to do is leave one of their stickers on a nearby fence and the horses and ponies are rapidly moved on. It is not legal but sometimes the frustration of landowners gets too much for them while they wait for local authorities to move the horses on, relying on court orders.

One difficulty is that fly-grazing laws differ in Wales and England and dealing with the problem is a low priority for cash-strapped local authorities. The worst repeat offenders try every trick in the book to dodge the penalties, such as saying the horses belong to another member of the family, but, happily, the courts are not deceived. Tom Price, the Welsh gypsy cob-breeder who was jailed in 2013 for 57 welfare and cruelty offences, was back in front of magistrates in October 2014 and found guilty of causing unnecessary suffering to 12 horses. He claimed the horses belonged to his son, Thomas, but he was not believed, sentenced to 32 weeks in prison, suspended for two years, and banned from keeping horses for five years.

WHW has always been involved with campaigning for tougher new laws but now we are pushing hard for the existing regulations to be enforced. It remains a long-winded legal process trying to move horses on after they have been dumped on private land. Something has to be done with the estimated 3,000 horses being illegally grazed in England. A private Members' Bill was finally introduced to Parliament in July 2014 by Julian Sturdy, MP for York Outer, aimed at matching the Welsh example, giving local authorities and also private landowners the power to seize horses abandoned without permission on private or public land. Some express concern that such horses will simply be 'culled', but which is better, a life of suffering, desperate for food, water and shelter, or a humane death? Until such a law is passed, landowners have a duty of care to the horses abandoned on their property until an owner can be traced, which strikes me as punishing the victim of the crime rather than the perpetrator. The reality is that fly-grazing is a long way down the list of priorities for budget-conscious government departments. I understand that from time to time it gets flagged up in DEFRA as a concern, no doubt because of intense lobbying by the likes of WHW, but it struggles to keep that attention. All that can be done is to keep on raising the issue.

What does it take to be a field officer? Horse knowledge, of course, is a crucial requirement; owners will very quickly find out if officers are unsure of themselves. They must be confident and have the courage to walk into the middle of travellers' camps. They will venture alone – supported by strict security protocols – into places most people would not dream of entering, whereas other charities will normally operate in twos or threes. It is not unknown for a field officer to be attacked and his car torched. This is not a role for the faint-hearted.

They also have to be capable of handling quite difficult horses which will not want to be loaded into trailers. Having rescued the horses, field officers also have to cope with the legal side, standing up in court to give evidence under tough cross-examination from defendants' barristers. Some of our officers are former policemen or are familiar with local authority issues. The charity also has investigators who may look at long-distance transportation routes and see how markets are operating; they build up chains of contacts across Europe.

A budget of £50,000 a year is allocated to each field officer covering salary, transportation and local call-out fees when a field officer requires a second opinion from a vet or if a farrier needs to called. The field officers often have to make difficult judgements. They know bringing a pony into one of our farms has cost implications but they cannot leave an animal in distress. Hall Farm in Norfolk, the headquarters of the WHW operation, costs £700,000 a year to run.

Probably the worst incident WHW was involved with was the Amersham case in 2008, described in court by the Recorder, His Honour Christopher Tyrer, as 'cruelty on a scale that beggars belief.' 31 horses, ponies and donkeys were found dead and more than 100 were removed from Spindles Farm, Amersham. The case, which ran from January 2008 until March 2011, was funded and prosecuted by the RSPCA.

Nick White was the WHW field officer first on the scene and his description of the chilling atmosphere he met at Spindles Farm is compelling: 'There were none of the normal noises I associate with a stable yard – horses moving about, eating, drinking, calling out to one another or the gentle noises that horses make when approached, expecting to be fed or cared for. They were totally silent. Even the horses that appeared in better bodily condition seemed to be depressed, almost as if they had lost their dignity.'

The owner of the farm, James Gray, was ultimately given a 26-week prison sentence and a life ban from owning and keeping horses. His family, including his wife, Julie, daughters Jodie and Cordelia and his son, James, were banned from owning and keeping horses for ten years. They appealed their convictions and the hearing dragged on, during which lengthy time only basic care could be given to the surviving animals.

It took two years from the time the case was first discovered until it reached appeal and the legal costs were horrendous; at one stage the RSPCA said the cost of caring for the horses and ponies that had survived their ordeal was £850,000. In starting a fundraising campaign to cope with the scale of the problem, Kirsty Hampton of the RSPCA said: 'This case was distressing beyond measure. What we were confronted with on arrival at the farm was grotesque... Many of the horses and ponies had just been left to starve and the smell of rotting flesh was overpowering.' Fighting the case all the way to appeal and the limit this set on how much could be done to help the rescued animals seemed like a deliberate ploy to prolong their suffering.

WHW took eleven of the horses into its Hall Farm. When the appeal was rejected, Roly Owers said: 'This was a simply horrific case, the worst in UK legal history, in which over thirty horses died. Thank heavens that after two long years, justice had been done and James Gray and his family have had their appeal quashed.

'Like all of the charities involved, the cost to care for the horses over the last two years has been enormous. We look forward to being able to find them loving new homes where they can look forward to a happy life far removed from the one they experienced in the hands of the Gray family.'

As I write, WHW has some 370 horses and ponies being rehabilitated and awaiting new homes at our four farms. We take in about 200 horses and ponies every year and have more than 1,600 rehomed; together with five other major welfare charities, we estimate that there are at least 6,500 that may need our help – this is the scale of a real equine crisis in the UK alone. Charities are being overwhelmed and Blue Cross, Horse Trust, British Horse Society, HorseWorld, Redwings, RSPCA and WHW believe England and Wales is in the grip of a growing horse crisis.

There are some worrying statistics

- RSPCA – took in 304 horses (April 2011–March 2012), twice as many as in the previous year;

- WHW – took in 326 new horses in 2013, a 76% increase on previous year
- Redwings – 28% increase from 2006 –2011; abandonments rose from 160 in 2009 to 450 in 2011.

The situation gets worse as economic difficulties suddenly make it harder for even responsible owners to cope; personal circumstances change as perhaps children outgrow their ponies or the weather deteriorates. Rain and snow very quickly turn paddocks into swamps and, while horses are hardy, they still need feeding, watering and protection from the worst elements.

Alongside the operational side of rescuing horses, WHW campaigns hard to change attitudes. One campaign, for example, is to ask people if they really do need to breed from their mares just because they are unable to ride or compete on them. We don't say, 'Don't breed', just 'Think first before doing so'. Although in earlier chapters I have mentioned the vast numbers of thoroughbred foals, charity research collectively indicates that twice as many foals are bred by people who will only breed 1–5 foals than by people who will breed more than 100 each. No one can be sure that they will be able to provide a home for their animals for life and our advice is to think twice before bringing yet another horse into an already overcrowded horse world.

The reasons some people give for breeding are varied and often mistaken. One reason is the belief that it can prevent laminitis, because increased hormones might somehow stop it. It doesn't. Laminitis is a major welfare problem in the UK because we have a vigorous grass-growing climate and too many fat horses and ponies in the country. Laminitis is not just a springtime problem, it can occur all year round; indeed, our research, conducted alongside the Animal Health Trust and the Royal Veterinary College in London, shows that June and December can be particularly bad times.

People don't give a second thought about going to a dog's home to find a pet but one of the last things people would do is come to ask for a horse at an equine charity. If they did so, it would allow us to increase the numbers we can help. WHW has countless stories of horses and ponies which have recovered and gone on to compete successfully or even just been a successful companion horse.

Not all of our horses are rescues, of course, as we take in mares that, unknown to us, are in foal. When that foal is born at one of our farms, it is given the very best care available. Its history and nutrition can be documented from the moment it is born and all it needs is bringing on and training. Conversely, if someone buys a horse through an advertisement, they will not know that it may be for sale because of a problem. When a horse or pony is rehomed from WHW, it will have received the best possible vetting and we give an honest appraisal of its ability. If a horse is a challenging ride, then it will only be rehomed to someone who is able to cope. Many of them are youngsters and capable of doing well.

There is also one other feature unique to WHW: no one actually buys a horse from us. They are only ever out on what we hope will turn out to be a permanent loan. In addition, there is full-time advice from our staff at the end of a phone and a twice-yearly visit from the charity throughout the horse's life. Should someone's personal circumstances change or if they run into difficult financial times, the charity will always take the horse back. It is a wonderful safety net and makes sense in terms of horse welfare as well as economically for anyone considering rehoming.

The Campaigns and International departments of WHW have changed dramatically over the years from what were once somewhat random – although effective – disparate operations. There are now full departments supporting the operatives in the field with set strategic objectives. A more targeted political approach is proving successful and the numbers of horses being transported has dramatically reduced from about 165,000 at the start of the century to around 60,000 in 2014.

These are some of the changes we want to see the government introduce in Britain:

- Change the law to allow swift seizure of fly-grazing horses or by making amendments to the Animals Act 1971
- Introduce legislation targeting fly-grazing – punishing offenders with fines and seizure of horses
- Introduce legislation or mechanisms to link better horses to owners to tackle irresponsible ownership
- Support local authorities with resources and the political will to tackle aggressive fly-grazing
- Encourage responsible breeding through guidance and education
- Provide more assistance for local authorities including provision of places to keep horses on a temporary basis
- Improve enforcement and co-operation between enforcement agencies and charities.

One of our hardest tasks, however, is probably to persuade governments to enact and, above all, enforce laws to bring an end to the live export of horses for slaughter; long distance transportation of horses destined for abattoirs is the single biggest abuse of horses and ponies in Europe. There can be no excuse for it beyond satisfying the stomachs of a few people. Maybe the first encouraging sign of a real breakthrough was the European Commission's first equine expert meeting in May 2014 in Brussels, where representatives from the equine sector, member states and welfare organisations concluded that there were several areas of welfare concern. It was hailed as a 'breakthrough in the wall of silence.'

Reineke Hameleers, Director at Eurogroup for Animals, said: '...it is clear that many more equines would benefit under the future Animal Welfare Framework Law or other dedicated harmonised EU legislation and implementation. This would ensure that actual law, soft law and educational effort go hand in hand and significantly raise the quality of life offered to Europe's equines.'

The difference between Britain and many developing nations is that the horse is now largely used for recreational purposes in the UK and is regarded as a companion animal, whereas it still plays a vital working role elsewhere. WHW is taking its campaign and philosophy around the world trying to educate and cajole; where it can get its message across, we are seeing immediate benefits.

8 | EUROPE

It took the discovery in 2013 of horsemeat in British beef destined for human consumption to focus minds on the plight of horses as they were, and continue to be, transported across Europe. It also enabled WHW to raise its profile by bringing the media's attention to a wide range of horse welfare issues. Every cloud does have a silver lining and this renewed attention has alerted both the public and those in government to what is happening to equines, despite legislation which is supposed to keep abuse in check.

Our President, HRH The Princess Royal, adroitly pushed the question into the headlines by quietly asking whether there should be more of a market for horse meat. Speaking at our conference in November 2013 she asked whether 'we should be considering a real market for horse meat and would that reduce the number of welfare cases if there was a real value in the horse meat sector?'

Laws exist governing the transportation of horses and ponies but, as our investigation in 2013 demonstrated, they are not being enforced, checks on the welfare of horses are not being made, the fate of these creatures is uncertain and their treatment en route undoubtedly cruel. Horses are not like farm animals and are ill-suited to being loaded en masse into lorries. Because of their higher centre of gravity, they need room to brace themselves, spreading out their legs and using their neck and head for balance, and of course they are fight or flight animals; when threatened or in unfamiliar surroundings they do not stand meekly together like a flock of sheep, so by the time they reach the end of a long journey, loaded closely together, there are always injuries. Horses are 16.5 times more likely to be injured during transport than are cattle (Stefancic and Martin, 2005).

There have been small victories along the way, such as the Tripartite Agreement (TPA) between the UK, Ireland and France, which restricted the free movement of horses and ponies between the countries to 'high health' horses including thoroughbred racehorses and breeding stock as well as FEI sports horses. However, the TPA was expanded in 2005 to allow all equids, except those being moved for slaughter, to move between the three countries without veterinary health certification. This loophole, which the WHW believes was allowing horses destined for slaughter to be transported across borders without checks, has now been closed to all but high health horses travelling to and from France.

Another benefit of the horse meat scandal was a renewed focus on the issue of the horse passport system, for which WHW has been pushing hard for some years. At last the European Commission and the UK's Department for Environment, Food and Rural Affairs (Defra) are looking again at equine identification. The WHW position is that all horses and ponies, regardless of age, should be micro-chipped so that they can be traced back to vets. Finally, in September 2014, it was announced by the EU Standing Committee on the Food Chain and Animal Health that, under new regulations, their information should be stored on a centralised database by 1 July 2016. WHW's Roly Owers welcomed the news: 'Horses in the UK will especially benefit from these tougher laws as the UK's system of equine identification could arguably be said to be one of the most complex and abused systems in Europe.' (*Horse and Hound*, 25 September 2014). These systems, though, cost money and it remains to be seen whether the 75 passport-issuing organisations in the UK alone can all be co-ordinated into one single effective database.

WHW is not an animal rights charity, it is an animal welfare charity, and we strive to ensure that what we campaign for is based on evidence. The equine identification programme is a typical example. It spearheaded surveys of nearly 3,000 horse owners and two abattoirs to evaluate their understanding of the regulations. 100 local authority enforcement agents, 600 vets and 54 passport-issuing organisations were also surveyed. The conclusion revealed a dramatic lack of confidence and shortcomings in most parts of the system meant to safeguard the human food chain.

The 2014 European Elections gave WHW another opportunity to promote horse welfare, coinciding as they did with the Chinese Year of the Horse. We tried to drive our points home in our own manifesto, campaigning in particular that:

- Horses need a much shorter journey limit when transported across Europe to slaughter
- Horses need an identification system that works
- Horses need their welfare and health protected in EU legislation
- Horses need the law to be enforced
- Consumers need food labelling that gives them the information to make welfare-friendly decisions.

This last point on labelling is important not just for horses, but also for consumers, who may have no idea where the meat they are buying comes from or how the animal was slaughtered. Horse meat may currently be labelled as a product of the country in which it was slaughtered, which could have no relation to where it originally came from or how it got to the abattoir.

While WHW accepts that eating horse meat is a personal choice, there are risks. Field investigations carried out by the charity between September 2010 and February 2011 examined many horses destined for slaughter and found that 93% of the animals in one shipment showed signs of clinical disease. There is great concern about the spread of equine infectious diseases such as equine infectious anaemia, which reappeared in Britain for the first time in 30 years in 2010, and the more virulent African horse sickness.

What is intolerable is the long distance transportation of 65,000 horses and ponies every year; most travel in inhumane conditions, with little food, water or rest, from Eastern Europe (45% from Poland, according to the *Daily Telegraph* of 24 February 2013) and Spain destined for Italy, the leading importer, France and Belgium. The giveaway to this largely illicit trade is the circuitous route taken by the lorries from Poland. Instead of going the more direct route through Austria, they add an extra 250 miles to the painful journey via the Czech Republic, Slovakia, Hungary and Slovenia before crossing into Italy. The reason is quite simply to avoid the more rigorous paperwork and welfare checks at the Austrian border. To reach their destination, drivers pass countless abattoirs which would at least alleviate the suffering from long journeys, but it seems the demand is for 'fresh meat'. (In America, where the last horse slaughterhouse closed at the end of 2006, it has meant a huge rise in horse exports, up 660 per cent to Mexico and 148 per cent to Canada, more than 140,000 in all per annum.) No one likes the thought of horses being slaughtered near their homes but the consequence of these closures means long-distance travel and prolonged suffering for the animals (ctpost.com, 5 April 2014)

ROMANIA

Horses are as vital to the Romanians as tractors are to British farmers. When I first visited Romania in October 2006 with Ian Kelly, then our International Director and the man who was largely responsible for standardising our overseas programmes, I was struck both by the numbers of working horses – there are probably a million or more – and by the desperate state of the roads on which they had to work; not only are they working animals, but for many people they are the only form of transport.

The initial focus of our work was Project Romania with our consultant farrier, Tom Burch, who had 30 years' service with the Metropolitan Police. It was a new approach with our Campaigns Department, covering veterinary, political and public awareness, working in tandem with International Training – farriery, saddlery and nutrition. It was a typical campaign conducted throughout the country, culminating in 2011. These projects were divided into three-weekly courses with separate training modules on shoeing and harness-making with on average a dozen students on each module. The duration of the course is to allow the students to return to work and continue providing for their families and, thankfully, they nearly all come back to continue their training.

The shoeing techniques there are traditional but primitive and, as the team found out, irregular. The horses may go for months without being shod and even when they are, it is usually a do-it-yourself process with rudimentary equipment and home-made shoes. Some only get re-shod when the shoe comes off. As Tom said, it requires a considerable degree of diplomacy to persuade people to modify their traditional techniques, but there is great enthusiasm to regain old skills which were lost during the Communist era when so many farm workers were sent to work in factories. Some of the students travelled 350 miles or more to attend our courses in Targu-Mures.

The students who undertook harness-making and saddlery were expected to bring their work back for assessment. The very best were then asked to work as paid assistant instructors for the following year so that they could pass on their new-found knowledge. Not only were we trying to improve skills among the ordinary farmers and workers, but we also worked with vets, teaching them practical aspects of horse care and nutrition. We ran courses on horse dentistry, head and neck problems and dermatology.

Tom Burch still returns regularly in a private capacity to Romania and while he sees signs of improvement, there is still a long way to go. Shoeing for many, he says, amounts to 'foot butchery' and takes two: the owner holds the foot up while the unskilled farrier hacks away with rudimentary cutting tools.

The concept of lameness is not understood by many in Romania or in a number of other developing countries. The owners have to be told that when they cut themselves they will have it treated; in the same way, if a horse is suffering, it too needs attention. In many instances, they believe the horses are mere animals and do not feel pain.

Farriery in Romania is not an industry. A horse's legs and feet are in fact regarded as 'dirty' and only looked at if absolutely essential. This means that even before a training course in farriery can begin, the basics of operating as a blacksmith must be mastered, turning whatever metal is available into shoes. The modest aim of many of these courses is to ensure that a shoe can be taken off safely, the foot trimmed safely and a basic, machine-made shoe replaced. This does not make them expert farriers but it does mean that some level of expertise is achieved and the very best students from a course will continue their training and in time become instructors themselves. Even with this skill, poverty is such that the newly-trained farriers cannot suddenly expect to make a lot of money, but they can trade their services for food while all the time improving the shoeing in their community.

In some countries, horses are shod, more often than not, while still attached to their carts. This upsets the balance and feet are cut at the wrong angle. Inevitably, the horse is lame when trotted away, and it remains that way for months until its next shoeing, the owner either oblivious or uncaring.

The focus on farriery and harness-making are fundamental to the welfare of the working horse. Some of the horses the charity sees are quality animals but are hobbling on 'Aladdin's Slippers' because no one knows how to trim feet. Eventually the fetlock joints ossify and, in the worst cases, there is nothing to do but put the horse down.

On the Campaigns side we worked closely with the Romanian government to promote the welfare of horses in the country and new laws have been introduced. More recently we have drawn attention to the long-distance transportation of horses from Romania. In one case our field officers, who would courageously attend these almost clandestine horse fairs at 2 or 3 in the morning, deemed 14% of the horses unfit even to begin their long journey to Italy; by the time they had reached their destination, it was estimated that 37% were in an unfit condition.

The whole animal transport question is hugely emotive and there has always been a great deal of public interest in it. WHW is not trying to be sensationalist and all our inquiries are above board and meticulously recorded. It can be a dangerous world, though; we suspect drug trafficking and organised crime are involved but no policeman is going to send his sniffer dog into a lorry full of horses. Some drivers carry guns, no doubt for their own protection but also to deter animal rights' activists. This is the world in which our field officers operate – some are female, relying on nothing more than a smile and charm to persuade the drivers and market owners at least to provide some water for the dehydrated horses.

Some might ask what the issue is: aren't horses used to travelling in lorries? In fact, most of these horses are not – they may never have been in a lorry, certainly not one as big as a transporter. Even for competition horses in prime condition, these journeys would be stressful. But these animals are either unfit through overwork and malnutrition or, at the other extreme, they have been fattened up for slaughter or have foals at foot. In any event, they are unable to withstand the rigours of such a long journey, tightly packed into a confined space. In hot conditions, horses struggle to regulate their body temperatures and so have a greater propensity to dehydrate than cattle or sheep. This happens quickly, within ten hours. This is too high a price to pay for a slice of Italian salami.

Jo White, the charity's former Campaign Director, undertook a number of visits to Romania, meeting everyone from the farmers who depend on horses for their livelihood, representatives from the Government, the university in Iași and the veterinary authority to those directly involved in the slaughter trade. In an article about the business she wrote: 'This is a complex and changing trade, where horses and their poor owners are used to making a profit. Romania is a prime target for the business man who is interested in making fast money...'

'Ian Kelly and I travelled to fattening farms and collection centres, which I can only describe as depressing beyond belief. Horses standing knee-deep in their own urine and faeces, waiting for the inevitable. Injuries are all too evident with ripped ears, infected cuts, swollen and filled legs.' (*Your Horse* magazine).

As ever, poverty and ignorance usually lie at the root of this suffering. Poverty, because people will do anything to make ends meet, and ignorance, because a lack of basic knowledge about horse welfare has been lost to generations. Some practices were brutal: to prove a horse's strength, a cart would be heavily laden, the brakes applied and the horse beaten to try and move the cart while prospective buyers sat in stands watching.

Wherever the charity conducts its projects, the aim is always to leave behind a sustainable infrastructure, particularly by training local people to share their newly-acquired knowledge; this was the basic principle established by Ian Kelly. An unexpected spin-off benefit of being awarded one of our certificates was that it entitled the recipient to priority housing. It amounted to a professional qualification and the same applied to our students in Africa.

It is also a principle that the charity will only go into countries where it is invited but we have no power to intervene where we see abuse, only to observe and report back. The desire to do something about horse welfare is not always matched by legal or official enforcement. In 2009, I was back in Romania and visited the Rădăuți stud farm, whose splendid buildings had seen better days pre-Communism but which now seemed sad and dilapidated. I saw about 200 horses, some of which looked as though they had not been handled, aged three or four, and some much older. They all stood in stalls, unable to move about, and many were in bad shape. I was told they were 'ready for meat' or would go to Italy. It struck me as being a bit rich that while we were trying to help them with their farriery, harness-making and general welfare, they were completely ignoring EU regulations.

On my return to Bucharest I boldly tried to raise the issue in a speech I was due to make at the British ambassador's residence. I had planned to say that the transport of horses from Romania's northern borders down to Italy was in contravention of existing EU regulations and I wondered if we could have help liaising with the Minister directly responsible for the national studs to stop sending live horses to Italy. I had also written in my speech that while we were training farriers and saddlers for the country, the transport of live horses was being ignored, and I considered that it was not a very 'fair exchange'. I was advised that the ambassador, Robin Barnett, who had generously hosted the reception for us, felt the draft of my speech was too strong. I toned it down but I suspect much was lost in the translation.

To ensure our efforts lived on, we announced a plan to develop a ten-year horse welfare strategy following the handover of Project Romania in 2010.

It seems that standards are improving. In the old stud farms there may still be posters on the walls showing precisely how the finest shoes should look, while in the same barns horses are left to stand in deep litter with their feet curling up. More often than not there may be no ventilation in the winter, in the mistaken belief that cool air might do horses harm. Yet slowly but surely, the number of animals waiting to be transported across Europe seems to be dwindling.

ITALY

Some 200,000 horses are slaughtered every year in Italy to satisfy the demands of the salami industry and 84% of the horse meat consumed in Italy is imported. (*Italy* magazine, 15 March 2013). According to the Italian Institute of Statistics, 51,653 horses were imported to Italy in 2010, 50,175 of which derived from other EU member states. It shouldn't make economic sense if the regulations governing the transport of live animals were being enforced, but of course they are not.

A report carried out by ILPH (WHW) into the economics of the trade in horses for slaughter from Spain to Italy as far back as 2007 showed that if the law (Regulation EC 1/2005) were being enforced correctly, journeys from southern Spain of more than 24 hours would become non-profitable, bringing to an end the long-distance transport of live horses from there.

Equally, enforcement should mean that shorter journeys of less than 24 hours should also be less profitable, because more vehicles would have to go out on the road in order to transport the same number of horses.

The report concluded that the carcass trade has the potential to become much more profitable than the live trade if the price of meat from outside Italy were more competitive.

What continues to this day is overloaded transporters, with inadequate separation between horses, driving for long hours with no rest breaks or adequate clean water. Most of these transporters head for the southern region of Puglia where in 2010 more than 31,000 horses were slaughtered. The argument is not against eating horsemeat, as we have said, but if Italians from Veneto to Puglia, Emilia-Romagna, Piedmont, Lombardy, Sicily and Sardinia were more aware of the origin of their salami and of the suffering that horses had endured to provide them with their meals, then perhaps the trade would stop and frozen carcasses could be shipped more profitably and more humanely.

IRELAND

Ireland was a perfect 'domestic' example of where charities like ours have to go about their business diplomatically, despite their very best intentions. Inspired by the Carew brothers Patrick and 'Bunny', WHW invested £100,000 in a study of the welfare issues in the island of Ireland, headed up by a very competent vet, Dr Joe Collins at University College Dublin (UCD). When I first visited in June 2007, I noted in my diary that we had to be careful not to tread on local toes. We highlighted in our discussion that there were clear differences in culture and controls, and working in Ulster in particular was not always easy. Some time later, when I attended an FEI meeting, the Irish representative even wondered why WHW was 'interfering'.

From the outset the two most critical issues were the disposal of horses and the treatment of horses at unregulated gatherings. In his report, Challenges and Solutions to Support Good Equine Welfare Practice in Ireland, co-authored by Dr Alison Hanlon, Professor Simon Moore, Professor Patrick Wall and Dr Vivienne Duggan from the UCD School of Agriculture, Food Science and Veterinary Medicine, Joe Collins warned that increasing numbers of horses were facing various risks, including being abandoned, exported or sent to abattoirs on economic grounds or as a result of 'oversupply'. The fact of the matter, as Joe's report observed in great detail, was that Ireland had, and probably still has, a problem. As ever with this sort of report, the fear is that its fate is to be left languishing forgotten on a dusty shelf.

The stories of people innocently buying one horse at a fair in Ireland and finding three unwanted horses or ponies coming out of the horsebox are legendary and still worryingly current. Joe Collins warned back in 2010: 'A key issue is the lack of a comprehensive system of registered ownership, including transfer of ownership, for horses in Ireland.'

'It is currently not possible to track horses from birth to death except those whose owners/keepers voluntarily register their origin, change of ownership, movement and ultimate demise,' he said.

'This has implications for equine health and welfare, including disease spread, the introduction of exotic disease, proper medicines use in horses and not being able to identify an owner/keeper to hold responsible in the event of problems such as the neglect or abandonment. Ireland needs better and stronger enforcement of horse identification at critical points such as at horse fairs and points of export/import.'

Particular concern surrounded the abattoirs. Licensed horse slaughterers at that time could only take horses if they had a passport. But passports were being issued to horses which were immediately slaughtered, thus circumventing the spirit of EU requirements. It was reported that instead of being slaughtered, some horses were being put back on the market and others transported live to Italy.

Even when Joe, Vivienne Duggan and their colleagues were conducting their research, it was clear that the routes of movement, sale and disposal of horses were not well documented or regulated. When tougher regulations were introduced, the terms could not be enforced and instead of making matters 'better' for horses, they were being shipped live over long distances, often ending up in Italy.

While it was rightly regarded as a world leader in equine-related activities from Connemara ponies to top-class thoroughbreds, the Celtic Tiger had been brought down by the economic collapse in 2008. It was obvious to Joe Collins and his colleagues by 2010 that 'horse production has outstripped demand in all sectors. This, coupled with the recent economic downturn, is one factor contributing to the escalating equine welfare problem.'

The report's authors also said that indiscriminate breeding of moderate-quality horses had compounded the problem of unwanted horses.

A key part of the Collins report looked at traveller groups. It was noted that while fairs, markets and impromptu race meetings were an acknowledged part of the traveller culture, there were, nonetheless, welfare issues. While accepting that standards of care and approach to horse husbandry differed from those of the 'settled community', it was apparent that there was a breakdown in the flow of horse knowledge within the traveller community from one generation to the next, and increasingly the newer generations were changing the type of horses they bred. They were introducing thoroughbred breeding to the stock in pursuit of greater speed at the expense of physical hardiness and stoic temperament.

I should just observe that the loss of 'horse knowledge' is certainly not unique to the traveller community; too often, people are acquiring horses without any such knowledge in the family and the consequences of what I call this 'equine illiteracy' are witnessed on a daily basis by WHW. That same illiteracy can be found in places like Romania, where whole farming generations were lost to the pursuit of industry, leaving their descendants with no first-hand experience. When WHW launched what it called its Root Causes campaign to find out why there seemed to be an increase in horse welfare issues in Britain, it had already identified a real decline in practical horse knowledge; much of the abuse is caused by ignorance as well as neglect.

Since 2010, the Department of Agriculture (DAFM) has introduced a requirement in Ireland that all those who keep horses register this fact with them, just as livestock keepers have herd numbers. This is motivated by a desire to know where horses are if an outbreak of infectious disease should occur. To encourage compliance, Horse Passport Issuing Organisations (HPIOs) now have to collect details of the Equine Premises Number when someone applies for a passport. DAFM has also introduced a central database to which each HPIO has to submit their horse registration information for central compilation, in an attempt to reduce double-passporting and fraud of other kinds. In addition, there is a legal requirement that there is 'transfer of ownership' of horses: if an owner sells a horse (and by law they must have a passport for each horse they own or keep) they must notify the HPIO of the change so that responsibility is transferred to the new owner/keeper. This is to make information on the passport much more current and relevant, and is useful if it becomes necessary to link an animal with an owner.

North or south of the border, cruelty continues. In December 2014, Robert McAleenan and his son Conor were jailed for what the judge described as 'one of the worst' cases of animal cruelty he had encountered. Police spoke of a 'scene of horror', with dead horses and ponies lying among living animals at the premises in County Antrim. Sixty-three were seized and nine were dead or had to be euthanased. Conor McAleenan claimed he had not given the horses medicine because he wanted to sell them into the human food chain. The two men were also banned from keeping animals for 25 years.

It is a key aim of WHW to grow its international side. While it is acknowledged that there will always be welfare cases in the UK and the work there is vital, what can be achieved by training a group of farriers or harness-makers in developing countries and teaching them how to be instructors is far greater in comparison for the same amount of effort. As WHW expands its work across the world, our single approach is to establish sustainability among farriers and harness-makers, as well as all horse owners we encounter, to leave behind a cadre of trained people capable of passing on a community-based approach to horse welfare. Where it is possible, we hope to train nutritionists and veterinary assistants but, as the following pages illustrate, no two countries are the same and not all will have the luxury of a veterinary university. How long we can maintain a presence in a country also varies. From an *ad hoc* country-by-country approach we developed a more focused five-year programme in each country, but even that depends on the circumstances we uncover on the ground. As always, we try and do what we think is best for the horses and ponies we find.

9 | INTO AFRICA

One of the most satisfying aspects of the work carried out by WHW in many parts of the world goes beyond the welfare of horses. My first visit to Cape Town was in 2007 to see the headquarters of the Cart Horse Protection Association (CHPA) which has been funded by a donation of £35,000 from the charity enabling it to erect its first permanent building. It is in the middle of commercial and industrial Cape Town, in what was once a rough area. A student told me that before the CHPA arrived, no one had dared even to walk along the street because it was so dangerous. Now though, because there were cart owners coming and going to the centre, there were more people about, carts loaded with scrap or building materials were trotting by all day, usually driven by young men or boys, and it was a much safer area.

Another morning, when we arrived at the centre, we found a man lying flat out on a trolley and I assumed that his condition was drugs-related. He had, in fact, cut himself. He had tried native remedies without success and now gangrene had infected his hand. In desperation the only place he could think of coming for help was the association's HQ. At that late stage, all the staff could do was ring for an ambulance to take him to hospital. It may only have been a minor incident but it demonstrated the remarkable impact this operation was having on ordinary lives in the city and the respect in which it was held.

Time and again the instructors and team leaders who work in so many different parts of the world say how rewarding it is to see the change in attitude among horse owners, who learn new skills and gain confidence as their training progresses. The students quickly recognise the difference they themselves can make in their own communities by improving the welfare of the horses which are so often essential to their livelihoods.

There is the other universal common denominator: the suffering these horses endure is often not from deliberate abuse but as a result of a lack of basic knowledge. Small changes can make an enormous difference and even where there is uncertainty and sometimes suspicion at the start of the training courses, they quickly turn to appreciation and a realisation that a healthy horse is a more valuable horse.

CAPE TOWN

My visit to Cape Town coincided with the final day of a farrier and harness-making course when 12 students were to receive their certificates. Their gratitude and pride at their new-found knowledge completely outweighed what our instructors had been able to teach them.

One of the students told me how he had been taught to sew on his own buttons and then progressed to being a harness-maker. 'I never thought I would be able to do this. I am so grateful for all the help I have received.' He was middle-aged and it was a new start for him in life. One of our group described them as 'second learners'.

The leader of the farriers spoke emotionally, in almost biblical fashion, about what he had learned, about the help he had received and how he would now go out and share the skills that he had perfected. This is precisely what the charity is trying to do wherever it operates in the world, creating a sustainable legacy which improves the lives of the population by helping and training them to look after their animals.

It was striking how much the people seemed to love their horses, which is not always the case in many countries, not least in the so-called civilised western world. While we were in Cape Town, a horse had been attacked by a swarm of bees and died, and the whole family came in to say their goodbyes.

Today, as its website (www.carthorse.org.za) proclaims, it 'boasts a farrier agency, harness shop, treatment stalls and paddocks, cart repair workshop, education and training room, administrative offices and a feed storage barn and provides services to over 500 working cart horses and their owners.' While I was there we visited a farm that the CHPA wanted to buy, emulating the work of the WHW and providing a base where horses could be rehabilitated out of the city. This is now flourishing, with stables, paddocks with shelters and an indoor arena as well as operating its own Adoption Programme so that people can rehome the horses.

Where possible, WHW tries to work with partners in countries where it might have the contacts but not necessarily the resources and technical support. As usual, it requires a good understanding of the country. It appears, for instance, to work better in Cape Town, where there is a manageable number of horses and a more European attitude towards horse welfare, than even Johannesburg, although here we have had some notable success too. In Cape Town they quickly picked up on the idea of having a rest place for their horses so that they could take them out of service for a time to rehabilitate

JOHANNESBURG

I went up to Johannesburg to visit the Soweto Equestrian Centre, established in 2008 in collaboration with the Soweto Equestrian Foundation and South Africa's first black show jumping champion, Enos Mafokate. Enos had worked for both David Broome and Anneli (Drummond-Hay) Wucherpfennig. When Ian Kelly had first visited the site strewn with debris and litter, it was derelict with ruined buildings. Working horses in the area lived and worked in poor conditions, pulling heavy carts of coal and scrap metal in and out of central Johannesburg; many of the horses actually lived in the coal yards. Their need was obvious. Enos subsequently spoke at our Annual Conference in London, still with a twinkle in his eye.

We were able to see one of the licensed coal yards where the horses were still in a poor condition: one of those with us managed to pull a staple out of a horse's foot. The carts were heavy, well below the basic standard one would hope for, and some of the wheels were buckled. The yard was a minefield for horses, with barbed wire and old tins and car tyres littered everywhere.

One of the team leaders, Des Bridges, described the challenge in those early days: 'The cart horses arrived and clearly showed the scale of the task to be undertaken. From ill-fitting harnesses and bridles causing deep sores in the mouth and around the breast, back and wither regions to horses being shod with re-enforcing bar (used predominately in the building trade), the problems faced were among the greatest I have seen.'

By the time of our visit, the Soweto Equestrian Centre had a clubhouse leased from the Johannesburg City Council, a large block of stables, an all-weather ring and fenced paddocks. Most importantly for our charity, we were able to use the centre as a base to teach farriery and harness-making under Ian's watchful eye. He had become something of a hero among the students, many of whom came for the presentation of their certificates all the way from Cape Town, Natal and Zimbabwe. Enos pronounced: 'There is God, there is Mr Mandela and there is Ian Kelly!' and he meant it.

LESOTHO

We travelled on to Lesotho, a wild and beautiful country entirely landlocked by South Africa. There is a rock inscribed with the words: 'Wayfarer, behold the Gates of Paradise', which it certainly is, in a rugged sort of way. It is a land which is increasingly attracting more adventurous tourists who can go pony trekking in the highlands, although our teams found that neither the largely novice riders oblivious to the state of their mounts, nor the ponies themselves, were really up to these long rides.

For most people the only means of transport is by horse (87,000) or donkey (147,000). There is also cattle and sheep farming but at the time of our visit only about seven vets in the whole country. This is a land where families are largely dependent on payments from men who cross the border into South Africa in search of work in the diamond mines and where three quarters of the population live in rural areas, eking out a living in subsistence agriculture. No real effort seemed to have been made to conserve water during the rainy season and, as a result of the ravages of HIV, there was almost a generation of male labour missing.

It took our teams several days to reach recruitment areas over narrow, unmade roads which had proved unforgiving to the occasional lorry that we found abandoned in the ditch, having failed to negotiate a corner. Having recruited students for the first module, the worry was always whether they would return for the next stage in their training. Barring accidents, they usually did, which was a testament to the impact the courses were having. Since the start of our project in 2007 we have trained 51 saddlers and 42 farriers.

On our visit we were taken to meet King Letsie III which, while being an honour, was also important publicity as the whole country would have known that he had taken the time to see us. This helped our credibility, although he was also interested in reminiscing with me about Cambridge.

As always, the tasks were rudimentary, helping students develop their cutting and stitching skills to make better-fitting saddles and demonstrating how to adapt rope halters to prevent injury to horses' mouths, but the additional help we were able to give was based on a very detailed preliminary study.

The WHW approach is always to adapt and modify its advice and training to suit local needs. In Lesotho, for example, before the start of the WHW training programmes, we were able to do this, having funded an in-depth study by Melissa Upjohn, a PhD student at the Royal Veterinary College, and her colleague Kristien Verheyen, into the specific issues facing horse owners in that country. We wanted to know what the horses were being used for, how they were being fed, if they were being vaccinated and how their tack was being maintained. The veterinary team, which included two locally-recruited research assistants, also examined many of the horses, including taking blood samples. Detailed discussions were held with owners who were able to rank their horse-care priorities and we could develop interactive educational workshops, including information on local feedstuffs in support of our farriery and tack-making courses.

What the survey found was that because of poverty and HIV Aids – life expectancy is around 52 years - among the subsistence farmers, vaccination was uncommon, worms were a major problem and almost all the horses tested were infested with intestinal parasites. Proprietary medicines were beyond the reach of most of the owners, who relied instead on herbal medicine, chilli powder, even Jeyes fluid and marijuana. Tack was basic and in poor condition, causing wounds on the withers and spines, and shoeing was a DIY effort using nails and shoes from hardware stores. Horse dentistry was essentially unheard of and if a horse had swollen gums, the traditional practice of making gum incisions with a knife to 'bleed' the gums was commonplace.

As an aside, WHW also insisted that the students had an HIV test, which not only ensured they remained well, but also drove home the importance to their daily lives of getting themselves tested, regardless of whether or not they were working with horses. The curse of Aids also meant traditions of farming and animal welfare which would normally have been passed from father to son and daughter were often lost. The line had been broken.

The horse owners, many of whom had heard of the WHW survey by word of mouth, all appreciated the opportunity to talk to experts with a technical knowledge and understanding of the day-to-day problems they faced. As a result, a more targeted approach was developed when the WHW training teams began their work. These baseline studies are now the first step in these projects to establish the most appropriate help we can offer; there is no point in talking about fitting the right shoes if no one can afford to buy them. Sometimes the first essential is to teach students how to make basic horse shoes from what is available locally. By the time I visited, the WHW courses were already having an impact and the newly-trained farriers were in high demand.

The harsh facts of life in a country like Lesotho changed one of our methods of working. New farriers and saddlers used to be given a brand new set of tools, manufactured in the west, to carry out their work. When students had financial problems or needed money to feed their families, though, the most valuable thing in their possession was usually the gleaming tool kit, which they promptly sold. To combat this and to ensure they kept the tools of their trade precisely to earn a living and care for horses, we arranged from then on for tools to be made locally and therefore more cheaply wherever we went, thus making them less of a temptation to sell.

WHW teams use every trick at their disposal to get the message of horse welfare across and a chance encounter with the Malealea Community Festival in Lesotho one year proved to be an irresistible opportunity, coinciding as it did with a farriery and harness-making course. It was a chance to reach a much wider audience of horse owners from the more remote parts of the country which our teams could not possibly access.

The Festival opened with a procession of 25 mounted Basotho horsemen and, with a captive audience of some 400 villagers, the students on the course were able to present in a combination of drama, dance and song the principles of acceptable animal welfare.

The Artistic Director of the Festival, Katt Lizzard, said: 'Working with World Horse Welfare enabled us to create a piece of theatre which focused on the role of the working horse in Lesotho.'

Our teams also tried new ways of combating the extreme drought conditions by developing a programme to increase food security for the malnourished working horses. They planted up 28 acres of feed crops in Malealea and Matsieng, which were distributed to the grateful communities. The rivers that carry all the water down from the mountains were dry. It would seem to have been easy enough to create dams to hold the water in spring, but the local leadership was not strong enough.

My conclusion at the end of my visit was that WHW would somehow have to keep up its support after our initial 5-year project and this probably needed to apply to other countries as well. Having acquired their new skills, the farriers and saddlers then had to run their own businesses, but as they were mostly illiterate that was always going to be a challenge. A specific Business Skills course was established, aimed at helping students realise the financial potential of their newly-acquired abilities. It was fairly fundamental, explaining how to devise a vision for the sort of businesses they wanted to run, teaching numeracy, how to budget, record keeping and, for some, even the basic use of a calculator. Another solution was to persuade the newly-trained men to get together from time to time, to keep in touch and compare notes on how they were getting on, enabling them to talk about and share their problems. By working together, forming groups based on their geographical locations, they could also share costs when placing orders for new equipment such as hide for the saddlery students. That principle has proved to be a success.

SENEGAL

Senegal is a small country in the extreme west of Africa, with a land area of almost 200,000 square kilometres and virtually surrounding The Gambia, where the charity had previously worked (2004–2008). Senegal is a deprived country where the working horse owners suffer from poverty, a lack of materials and basic skills. At the start of a five-year initiative in 2008, WHW soon established that better hoof care, tack and nutrition were the priorities but, as usual, solutions had to be practical and locally sourced where possible.

There are around half a million working horses in the country and virtually all the ones we saw were underfed, suffering from ill-fitting tack and regularly battered by poorly-designed carts, many of which were no more than cannibalised car axles. The shafts were often made out of a single scaffolding pole cut in half without a swingle tree, which meant that they jabbed into the horses' sides as they tried to manoeuvre. The shoes were usually made from light reinforcing steel rods from building sites, and always badly fitted, the hoof having been made to fit the shoe rather than the shoe shaped to fit the hoof. The only proper shoes were expensive and imported for use by the police and wealthy horse owners.

One solution to the shoeing problem was a manual horseshoe-making device designed by master farriers and named the 'Tommy'. The hope was that this would allow local farriers to make cheaper and more durable shoes. The first group of 20 students, some already working as self-taught farriers and harness makers, came from different backgrounds but lacked both the equipment and knowledge to carry out their work effectively or, indeed, to keep their horses healthy. One horse arrived with bad sores which the well-meaning owner had decided to treat with dry cement powder. The course took place in Dakar, the capital city, where there were twice as many horses and carts as there were cars.

The injuries from the carts was another challenge but the solution was the so-called Hula cart, a lightweight design built in the country and costing £500, funded by WHW donors. I presented the first five to Senegalese workers whose livelihoods depended on their horses. Hula carts can now be seen in other parts of the world, bearing plaques attached as a permanent reminder of generous donations from WHW supporters.

Following our visit and on the advice of Dr Fall, then Minister of Horse for Senegal, WHW decided to open a new training centre in Louga, a district with some 3,000 horses, where we were given a very noisy welcome and a triumphal ride in a cart. Such official recognition is really important and, wherever possible, the red carpet was rolled out for us on such occasions, with African vets dressed in brilliantly coloured native costumes; in fact, on one occasion the whole prize-giving ceremony had to be repeated – complete with the red carpet - to enable the cameras to capture the relevant minister actually handing over the certificates. To date, WHW has trained 40 farriers and saddlers and is working with other stakeholders in the country as well as the veterinary department of the University in Dakar that receives students from 15 other African countries. The Senegalese typically live in close-knit communities, so the farriers and saddlers trained by WHW can easily share their knowledge with the farmers, the men who use their carts as taxis and all horse owners, advising them about the importance of maintaining their horses' feet and ensuring that harnesses and tack are properly fitted. If the horse goes lame and cannot work, it means no income for the family. No hoof, no work.

Having concluded its final training module, the charity now concentrates on supporting the government-based training scheme and developing a community-based approach for equid owners in and around the town of Rufisque in the Dakar region of western Senegal.

THE GAMBIA

Amid all the suffering, it is good to highlight a success story. Since the charity began work in The Gambia in 2004, our trained farriers have been having an impact, none more so than Baba Trewelly. Such was his ability that he went on to become an assistant trainer in the country and acted as Regional Training Advisor in neighbouring Senegal. The only thing holding Baba back was having to borrow his brother's pushbike to reach his growing clientele. Thanks to the generosity of WHW sponsors, we were able to buy him a motorbike so he could reach even more horses and donkeys to care for their feet.

Others have called for more research into the value of working equids, dubbed 'the missing link', in so many developing economies. There is a need to convince governments and policy makers that donkeys and horses are making an important contribution which can actually be quantified in real monetary terms.

Governments in developing countries can be embarrassed about having to use donkeys to transport goods and yet they are the invisible link delivering crates of aid in times of disaster. They are, indeed, the invisible link for one billion of the poorest people in the world as they struggle to survive in their daily lives. Rather than be embarrassed, governments should recognise the value of these animals and the contribution which they make. They are often overlooked and are never given credit for the work they do and yet without them, the first step in that first mile of reconstruction could never be made, those crops gathered in would be valueless without a donkey or horse to haul them, sometimes miles, from field to market place. When WHW and The Brooke, another leading equine charity, speak about the importance of helping horses, donkeys and mules, they want the rest of the developed world to recognise that by doing so, they are not just helping to improve the lives of the animals, but that they are making a real, even dramatic, difference to people's livelihoods. The key message from charities and the concerned public to the policy makers is this: that when they are making their life-changing decisions, they should remember the role of the working equids.

Speaking at the 7th International Colloquium on Working Equids, hosted by WHW in July 2014, Delphine Valette of The Brooke described the relationship between working equids and women in particular in countries like Ethiopia, Kenya, Pakistan and India. She said they ranked equids first among all their animals because they depended on them for their chores, carrying firewood and water. Donkeys were a physical benefit, saving the women from back-breaking tasks, particularly during pregnancy, and they were income generators, especially in women-headed households. Donkeys were flexible, able to carry goods or plough a field, depending on the season, and the income they generated paid for food, healthcare and education. She quoted one woman: 'The donkey affects each and every aspect of my life as a woman. On a typical day the donkey fetches water which I use to do the laundry, to do the dishes, to clean the house and for bathing. It also collects wood which I sell to buy flour for the evening meal. In other words I eat, drink, dream of the donkey and also, as a woman who is not employed, I work hand in hand with the donkey. The donkey is like me but, to put it plainly, the donkey is me.'

Now imagine the scene where there is no donkey to carry out these tasks. The family then really do fear for their survival; they have to cut down on what meagre food they have, the women have to carry the heavy loads themselves and if they are pregnant they can and do lose their unborn child. As Delphine put it, donkeys are not just vital to the family, they are part of the family, like another limb.

WHW President, HRH The Princess Royal, addressing the Colloquium, which was attended by more than 150 delegates from 28 countries, said: 'Animal welfare is just as important as child welfare in the context of human welfare in developing countries depending upon the welfare of their horse. The horse's welfare is paramount because it is the horse which carries the child to his place of education or fetches the water for the family in place of the child, which enables the child to go to school. The horse carries the child to medical attention should he need it, carries the mother to hospital while in labour and carries the vital food supplies so that mother can carry baby on her back instead of leaving baby alone at home.

'There is a real scope for animal welfare organisations to work together with human development organisations if we can work out how to get across to the more sceptical audience the value of the working animal to communities in the long-term.'

What is happening in Africa matters in Western countries as well. As I have already mentioned, African horse sickness is widespread and countries like Ethiopia, with the largest working equid population on the continent – nearly 10 million horses, donkeys and mules – suffer from a multitude of infectious diseases including epizootic lymphangitis, strangles, tetanus and ulcerative lymphangitis. Nigatu Aklilu of the Society for the Protection of Animals Abroad, another speaker at the WHW Colloquium, reported: 'African horse sickness is prevalent in almost all areas where horses are owned in Ethiopia and its impact is devastating. The new vaccine produced by the National Veterinary Institute has proved highly successful. However, there are still many reported outbreaks and mortalities amongst unvaccinated horses.'

As usual, it is often the lack of information among horse owners about the importance of vaccination which allows these diseases to spread and arrive on European shores.

Mass transportation to slaughter, from Romania to Italy

Brutal loading technique, Hungary

The Hon Gerald (Bunny) Maitland-Carew (left), former ILPH chairman with the author

HRH Princess Haya of Jordan at WHW Conference

HRH The Princess Royal launching Rehoming Campaign

How Catalina was found in San Pedro Sula, Honduras (left) and, right, Catalina after care

Above: The author presents new Hula Carts, Senegal

Below: Dartmoor Pony Sales; an auction of mares and foals at Chagford

The team at the 'Dallas-style' feral ponies round up, Scotland

Sharney as she was found and right, after months of care

Above: Chief Executive, Roly Owers, getting to know a new arrival

Below: WHW welfare team, Soweto

Farriery training, Guatemala

Left: Mare and foal, Soweto

Right: There was nothing to eat or drink at the former Romanian National Stud

Horse market, Mexico

The Jockey Club morning room

10 | LATIN AMERICA

In any one year, WHW may be conducting some 400 days of training in countries around the world. The aim in the relatively short time we have available in any country or even any district is to train as many students as a course will allow, reach and treat as many horses, ponies and donkeys as possible to show the right way to care for these hard-working creatures and to leave behind a programme of activity to ensure that the welfare work continues. It can seem a daunting task.

MEXICO

The charity first started operating in Mexico in 1991 and, exceptionally, it is still there, as it is such an enormous country and a useful engine room to power us into the rest of Latin America.

In Vera Cruz, the poorest state in Mexico, there are probably 400,000 horses, donkeys and mules. When word gets out that WHW is conducting a clinic in a village, together with The Donkey Sanctuary who partner with us, the locals usually turn out in strength with a string of animals all needing some sort of treatment. On our visit there was proof, if any were needed, of the legacy of WHW's work, with past students, now assistant instructors, sharing their knowledge. They were all not only happy in their work but rightly proud of what they were doing; one had made a special rack for his tools which I saw him cleaning with great care at the end of the day.

There were no such happy scenes at the San Bernabe Market in Mexico City where one of our party loosened the rope on a cow which was being strangled. Here again, The Donkey Sanctuary had provided shedding with a proper water supply for the countless horses, ponies, donkeys and mules. Every type of living creature seemed to be there, from piglets and chickens to rabbits and fighting cocks with spurs.

We found one horse that had been shot in a lorry by the WHW representative vet who had discovered it with a broken hip. By the time we got there, the wretched animal had already been gutted and its body was hanging by the side of the truck, waiting for the full load of live horses to go off for slaughter. At the same time other horses were being loaded viciously into a two-level transporter and it came as no surprise to hear a couple of the horses fighting and kicking inside.

By contrast we found pens with one or two well-groomed horses. The owner, if that is what he was, had driven for 40 hours from the United States and was asking £20,000 for them. Whether the horses really belonged to him or not, at least they seemed to be in good condition despite the ordeal of their journey.

On a brighter note, WHW established a close working relationship with The Donkey Sanctuary and the huge university in Mexico City – Universidad Nacional Autónoma de Mexico (UNAM). They take 500 students for six years and so have 3,000 vets on their books; it is the only veterinary school in Mexico, so there must be a substantial demand for places. This joint project has meant WHW trainee farriers and saddlers have been able to work alongside UNAM veterinary teams and learn the importance of developing a positive working relationship in their respective specialities.

Sometimes the solutions can be modest, even cheap. WHW found in some parts of Mexico that the horses were dropping dead from dehydration as they carried loads out to waste dumps. The answer was to provide buckets for the children who would charge the equivalent of a penny to water the horses. Not only did it provide a new income for the family but, crucially, it offered hydration for the horse, and all that was needed was a few buckets. There was no point shipping in expensive equipment which could neither be afforded nor replicated locally, as we had discovered with the farriers tool sets.

GUATEMALA

To watch students eagerly taking in the information offered by the WHW saddlery and farriery instructors while sheltering under a tree beside a river is a sight to behold and it shows how much they want to learn. Guatemala is a mountainous country with some 510,000 working equines, mainly in the central and northern regions and, like so many of its neighbours, wracked with poverty. As usual the population living in the rural communities depend heavily on their horses and donkeys to get about, transporting crops through the dense forests to market. It is a tough existence for both.

The country also highlights one of the key challenges facing WHW when it arrives for the first time in a new country. There are 28 different languages and therefore 28 different sub-cultures in Guatemala. In addition, there is a rigid social structure in each of these communities which has evolved over 150 years or more, and learning is by practice rather than by any formal academic system. It is fundamental that we need to work with the cultures we find, rather than try to impose a 'one solution fits all.' Every country, even every different community within a single country, requires a specifically designed approach.

For this reason WHW adopts an holistic approach to its support, as well as teaching the basics of equine care. It seeks to do this precisely because it can help the social and, ultimately, the economic prospects of the region and it backs up its work by talking to governments, seeking to get them to introduce new laws and directives to support those living in rural communities who so often are the backbone of these countries. The charity seeks to link horse welfare to livelihoods, not to try and mould livelihoods to fit the welfare on offer.

WHW first worked in Guatemala in 2006 when the charity launched four courses in Jalapa and trained 40 local farriers and 40 saddlers, greatly assisted by being allowed to use buildings on an army base supported by a local vet. When I visited, I was struck by the way they eagerly shared their new-found knowledge, proudly showing well-made harnesses and saddle packs. On one occasion when I was asked to present the prizes and certificates, a student came up to me and offered me a head collar which he had made. He said he wanted to thank us for all the help we had given him. I was proud to accept the gift on behalf of the charity and it brought home the impact we were having in a small way on so many people. By being able to make his own tack and by being able to sell his services on to other equine owners, his entire family would have a better life.

In order to reach as many working horses as possible, the teams then moved to Chimaltenango, 35 miles west of Guatemala City; leaving an area is always a difficult moment but WHW has to spread itself thinly to get the message across.

Our instructors also established a nutrition programme with plantations of Swazi grass, forage sorghum and alfalfa - the better fed the horse, which hopefully was now also better shod, the more productive it would become; as far as possible, WHW tries to encompass the needs of the horses' diets as well as improving their feet and saddle bags in its training.

Word quickly spread whenever WHW was in an area – sometimes just working on an open barren strip of land – and horse owners would soon be lining up. Shoeing and tack repairs were free and one apparently novel idea, which always guaranteed a big audience, was the advisability of castration. This 'new introduction' always created a stir and a crowd of enthusiastic onlookers of all ages who spent most of the day watching the vets. These operations were 'all part of the service' while WHW was working there.

This was also an opportunity to work with soldiers who, having completed their national service, were learning agricultural skills to help them adjust back to civilian life. At least these students now also had the additional knowledge of basic equine care which they could pass on.

Six years later we were back, this time in the Zaragoza region of the country, providing a comprehensive training programme aiming to reach as many of the 1,100 equine population as possible. Sadly we found the usual catalogue of ill-fitting harnesses, misshapen hooves as a result of poor shoeing skills and generally wretchedly miserable horses and ponies. Once again it was not a case of abuse but just of a lack of knowledge and resources. The aim, as ever, is to leave behind a sustainable programme of healthcare with Community Based Equine Advisers (CBEA) available to educate and inform all horse owners. In time, everyone in Guatemala should at least have heard that there is a better way of looking after their horses.

By 2014, WHW was running its first fully regional lead training course in the country with purely Guatemalan instructors who had completed their own studies. Periodically, UK instructors visit to assess the progress of instructors and students and to offer further guidance. This of course is the ultimate aim for every country in which the charity operates. They need to become self-sustaining to ensure the long-term welfare of working horses.

HONDURAS

Since 2010, WHW has been working in Honduras where there are some 100,000 working equids. As there are on average six members in every family, that means 600,000 people depend on these animals for their income and survival.

Since 2013 the charity has been running a project in the Choluteca region, having been told that as many as 2,000 cart horses were suffering working long days in ill-fitting harnesses pulling heavy loads and with little adequate food.

In common with many rural districts, there was a lack of services and products for equine owners. The only farrier WHW could find when it first went into the area was in his eighties and partially sighted and, as a result, shoeing was a do-it-yourself task using basic tools and limited skills. The only available 'new' shoes that WHW researchers could find were a one-size-fits-all in a local market. Once again, hooves were being shaped to fit the shoe and horses, inevitably, were suffering.

A WHW study showed that on average the horses travelled 15 kilometres a day, working five hours a day, six days a week. Urban horses usually worked more as they were also involved in government-run waste collection programmes. Rural horses were mostly involved in collecting firewood, the primary source of income, as most of the region was without electricity.

Debbie Warboys of WHW told me that she and her researchers established that the income-generating power of a working equid was the equivalent of $10 per day but most families of six had to survive on a total of $15 per day and even that was clearly not enough. While they all recognised the earning potential and therefore importance of their horses to their livelihood, it was usually a case of the family's needs taking priority over those of the horse. Debbie remembered one horse owner who said he tried to save $2.50 per day for his horse because he realised that if he managed to set that money aside he could feed the animal, trim his feet and, over 45 days, replace the entire set of harness. He was a shining example.

The vital role that working horses play in the economy for 80% of the population is self-evident and yet they face a lifetime of suffering unless standards of care can be improved and, critically, unless knowledge about the welfare of their most prized possession can reach more people, particularly the young. To reach as many horse owners as possible, locally- trained horse owners have become CBEAs. They have all been given in-depth coaching on equine husbandry and healthcare and serve as the link between other horse owners and the service providers.

Along with the farriery and saddlery programmes and instruction on how to make the best use of locally-available material such as sacks, straw blankets and soft rope, WHW teams have been allowed into village schools and performed pantomimes about the cart horse and its role in their society. This is to encourage the next generation of horse owners to appreciate the importance of treating their horses and ponies well and of keeping them healthy.

In partnership with The Equitarians, an American association of voluntary equine vets, immediate health care has been provided and WHW has lobbied government officials to try and extend the support given to urban horse owners to the rural community; if the waste recycling programme were extended out into the country, it would provide a new income- generating stream and therefore more money to spend on the horses as well as more food on the family table.

COSTA RICA

Another project was launched in Costa Rica where WHW was told that 600 horses had been suffering from preventable injuries and poor footcare. 'Poor' is an understatement because, with no farriery service available, horse owners resort to hacking away at hooves with machetes, a technique apparently handed down through the generations. The result, of course, is often misshapen feet when too much hoof is cut away, despite the obvious pain the horses have to endure when they carry on working.

WHW found that there were two veterinary stores at the border but for those living in Guaymi village, 35 kilometres away, it was simply too far. To reach a vet would have taken another 30 kilometres. Even in a modern town, a horse owner might think of trying to make do without having to drive a 130-kilometre round trip, but think of doing that on unmade tracks and possibly even on an already unsound horse. No wonder they reach for the machete.

HAITI

When the 2010 earthquake hit Haiti, the poorest nation in the western hemisphere, with a magnitude of 7.0 on the Richter scale, 220,000 people lost their lives and half the population was left homeless. Some years after the event, thousands are still living in makeshift accommodation without electricity or water. Against such destruction and loss of life it is easy to forget the animals, but they suffered too. By 2014 most of the island was still struggling to regain something approaching normality. It was into this chaos that WHW stepped to offer help to the horses, donkeys and mules that were playing such an important part in rebuilding the country, working with Humane Society International, the US-based animal welfare organisation, already on site, and partnered with The Equitarian Initiative.

In fact donkeys are the primary form of transport but there is limited access to material or knowledge on how to look after them. Rudimentary saddle packs cause pressure sores and wounds to the withers and backs; people put coats and blankets over the wounds because they think that will be easier for the donkey, when it might be making matters worse. They do not mean to hurt the animal, indeed they think the world of it, but lack of knowledge, resources and opportunity mean that animals' welfare is compromised.

'Working equids are being used to transport goods to market and to transport building materials as the work of rebuilding Haiti's property and roads continues,' said Liam Maguire, director of international operations at WHW. 'These horses also play a direct role in the welfare of many families who rely on them to make a living.'

Liam explained the stark reality behind working in many of these countries: 'These are largely working horses and they are never going to be anything else. You are not going to be able to put them in green fields to live out their days because that is simply not acceptable to their owners, to their economies, so we have got to focus on making their working situation better, helping their owners understand the benefit of welfare to the horses. You don't have to be a Horse Whisperer to see that horses would work better if their feet were looked after and harnesses fitted. Just trying to teach them to consider the horse's feeling, which does not come naturally to them, is a first step.'

Karen O'Malley, WHW's Head of Programme Development, remembers that in Honduras the owners were amazed that our people would go up and stroke the horses, talking to them and asking the owners what their names were. By the end of two weeks, though, those people were doing the same and giving the animals names because they saw that the people taking these attitudes had a way with horses. In some countries, though, they look on horses as we might look on an old Transit van. These people are afraid of horses, they are big animals, but then they would see small women from our teams going up to them, stroking them and talking to them, with the horse reacting and doing what that person asked rather than trying to bite them. They were impressed by that.

Liam added: 'In Nicaragua they felt from a religious point of view that it was wrong to put a horse down so what they would do is abandon them in ravines and wait for the floods to carry them away. That attitude was very deep-set so getting them to change was a challenge. We had a similar experience in Cambodia.'

'In Guatemala we found a horse with a broken leg. The owner was a member of the horse owners' association and that was a thing of pride for her, a status symbol. So if the horse was put down she could not stay a member; the horse was in a very bad condition.

'People vary the world over. The way they behave might depend on their situation. Generally people who have working horses in these countries are at the poorer end of the spectrum so if they do something for the horse, something has to be lost somewhere else, perhaps by cutting back on the food they can put on the table. What they can do is often constrained by those practical economic circumstances rather than what they know. Even if they recognise that the horse needs to be seen by a vet, there may not be any and if there is a vet, they may not be used to treating large horses. So what you are dealing with is based on a lot of factors.'

Roly Owers summed it up: 'You are always going to be upset about what you see in some of these countries and the day you stop getting upset you should retire or give up the job. Clearly standards in the UK and somewhere like Nicaragua are very different but the standard for people is very different too. You don't accept it but you try and understand it and you use that understanding to drive the programmes that we run.'

11 | THE LAW AND EDUCATION

The welfare of animals has to begin with education – the law can only do so much. There are two levels of education: one in the developed world, where there is every opportunity to own and care for horses and ponies for sport or as pets, and the other in the developing world, where owning a horse or donkey may make the difference between surviving or not surviving.

In the first instance the onus is on the parents and schools to set the standard. In all probability, those reading this book will need no persuasion that it is the duty of everyone who owns a pet to recognise that it is a privilege which carries with it responsibilities. In the case of a horse, those responsibilities are considerable and difficult to sustain every day, throughout the year, even when the rain is beating down.

It may seem old fashioned but I believe that some children have 'never had it so good,' as Prime Minister Harold MacMillan told the country back in 1957 when England was enjoying boom times. Some children today are enjoying the good times with their parents doing far too much for them when it comes to caring for their ponies. Mucking out a stable is heavy work but at least children should show willing. Even if they have not yet got the strength to lift a hay bale, even the smallest tots can brush down a Shetland pony and do their bit to tidy up the yard.

This book, though, of course, is about graver concerns than the typical idle teenager more interested in their iPhone than doing the chores. Looking after an animal, as well as being educational, can help lay the foundations for becoming a caring individual. An RSPCA survey found that 95% of school teachers said children would benefit from animal welfare education because it would make them more compassionate and socially aware. 83% of the teachers surveyed believed animal welfare should be part of the curriculum.

WHW also backs the idea: 'Education is essential to tackling the root causes of welfare problems in the UK and worldwide. Most welfare problems we see are not due to cruelty, but to a lack of basic horse care knowledge', said Sam Chubbock, WHW's Deputy Head of UK Support. (*Horse and Hound*, 12 June 2014)

'At our centres, we encourage children to learn about what horses need to thrive. We work closely with a secondary school in Blackpool to teach animal care as part of its curriculum.

'There's a surprising number of skills needed to care for a horse, especially numeracy when weighing out feed, or weighing and measuring horses to ensure a healthy weight.'

It is, for example, ignorance which lets people leave their litter behind when they visit the wonders of Dartmoor, as horses are undiscerning about what they eat and it is no help to the ponies if the public hand out unsuitable food. The ponies have been a feature of the moorland for 3,500 years; during industrial times they were used to haul loads from the tin mines. All ponies on Dartmoor today are privately owned by farmers who let them graze freely. The tragedy today is that there is little demand for the ponies and they are breeding faster than they can be sold – a programme of putting mares on the contraceptive pill is having an effect but there are probably still far too many stallions, although the actual numbers on the moor have dropped from more than 25,000 in the 1930s to fewer than 800 today. Even the markets of meat for the continent are being undercut by cheaper foreign suppliers and, sadly, hundreds of ponies have to be shot each year. It is a delicate balancing act to continue to use the ponies to graze the moorland and preserve its features while ensuring that their numbers are controlled.

With WHW field officer, Jeff Herrington, I attended one of the 'drifts', when the ponies are rounded up towards the end of every year to be sorted, their health checked and some sold; there were hundreds of pens with mares and foals or young stock, being sold for sometimes as little as £5 a head. When I asked what would happen to them, I was told they would go to the local zoo to feed the lions. The reality is that there are far too many pony stallions. Somehow that level of uncontrolled breeding has to be stopped, for the sake both of the ponies and for the moorland. The question is why this is now a problem and I suspect the answer, in part, is because there are fewer farmers working the land; in the past they would simply have taken the matter into their own hands. I don't suppose it is quite so easy or acceptable for them to reach for their rifles these days. We all want to see the ponies roaming freely on Dartmoor, Exmoor and in the New Forest – it attracts tourism and it is good for the local economy – but dig a little deeper, look a little harder and it is not long before difficulties and concerns emerge. As usual, it comes down to man and animal trying to live in harmony.

The tragedy is that the pure Dartmoor pony is actually in serious decline. Cross breeds – the ponies we usually see because the pure-breds are too valuable to be allowed to roam – are of little value, as we have noted. I suppose the question is whether anyone cares enough about them to preserve this symbol of Dartmoor?

Does anyone want to bother understanding? In September 2014, the Dartmoor Hill Pony Association (DHPA) proposed the unthinkable, for some: that the ponies should be bred for meat, to save them from disappearing from Dartmoor altogether. Inevitably, that provoked outrage. Becky Treeby of the South West Equine Protection group said: 'We will never support overbreeding or killing ponies for profit.' But the statistics make bleak reading. Of 900 foals born each year, 30% are homed, 10% go back in replenishing the herds and 60% are shot (*Horse and Hound*, 2 October 2014).

Jeff, who has been working the moors since moving to Devon in 1975, says the original Dartmoor pony was crossed with the Shetland specifically to work the mines, so the gene pool was changed. Pure-bred Dartmoors can still command a reasonable price. He noted that new regulations about methods of transportation, the requirement for passports and micro-chipping have unwittingly affected the market for sales to Ireland. Ponies had to be individually boxed for their journey on the ferries, which meant it was uneconomic for the Irish buyers to attend the sales. You may be able to buy a pony for £5 but there are additional costs to pay before it can be moved. The intentions behind new legislation may have been good, but its impact has not been entirely so.

Chagford is the only pony sale left in Devon. Jeff attended what may be one of the last sales, which ran at a loss for the auctioneers, Rendell. Half of the 250 ponies failed to find a buyer and, said Jeff, their fate was to be returned to their farms where they would probably be shot. This is not the picture holiday makers like to see, but if Dartmoor wants to remain a tourist attraction it may be incumbent on the National Parks to help find a long term solution. No ponies would mean fewer tourists and the ecology of the moorland itself would then suffer.

But there is another worry about an area which fails to attract as much publicity as the better known Dartmoor, Exmoor and New Forest: Bodmin Moor in north-eastern Cornwall. Jeff fears that Bodmin, which is actually a collection of 25 small moors with no one organisation in charge, has become a 'dumping ground' for horses and ponies. He knows that Arabs, quite unsuited to the sometimes harsh conditions of the moors, are abandoned there and are unable to survive. All equine charities are concerned that after a couple of mild winters, the UK is overdue a freeze.

When things go wrong, and well-meaning individuals who cannot stop 'rescuing' horses and ponies themselves become welfare issues, it's due to a kind of sickness, an inability to see the suffering they are causing to the very creatures they say they love so much. All that can be done in such cases is to hope that the general public realises that such herds are not something to be admired from afar as they drive past in their cars. Education in this instance is more about awareness : does the ground look poor ? Is there any grass in the field or is it all mud and brambles? Can they see any water for the horses and ponies to drink? This does not require any 'horse knowledge', just a little common sense. The real problem, I suppose, is that we are all worried about interfering – 'It is none of our business!' – and even fearful of the threat of retaliation from landowners. Charities like WHW and the RSPCA have highly-trained and sensitive field officers who are skilled in handling the most complicated and even potentially dangerous situations, so all it takes is a call to one of their helplines.

After illness and ignorance, the problem becomes one of crime. Over-breeding, as we have seen in Wales, where coloured ponies were once so prized, means that they are now devalued and consequently neglected. The breeding continues unabated in pursuit of that elusive winner but the vast majority never make the grade and are abandoned under motorway flyovers or on any convenient patch of ground. That is where the law must step in and where government must make it easier to prosecute, rather than be led a merry dance with appeal after appeal extending the suffering of horses and ponies. A horse whose ribs are protruding, whose hooves are curling over – the 'Aladdin's Slippers' effect – or who has not got the strength to lift his head or put one painful foot in front of another, has been abused. Slow justice is no justice for these creatures and surely all parts of the British Isles should be in support of the option that it be humanely put down without any recourse to the law. If owners cannot look after their animals properly, they should forfeit the right to keep them.

Like it or not, the United Kingdom is part of the European Union and our borders are wide open. This, however, should not mean that we turn a blind eye to what is happening in the underworld of long-distance transportation. If laws are passed to regulate such movement, they should be rigorously enforced and where they are not, there should be penalties not only for the transport companies and the dealers in their clandestine fairs but also for the governments which allow such trade to go on within their own borders. The laws exist but they are either being flouted or, as we have noted, are simply going unenforced, which surely makes a mockery of the whole legal process.

What should the police do if they find a lorry crammed full of suffering horses at a border crossing? Should they turn them back, which does nothing for the horses? Should they seize the horses? What would they do with them? Who will take care of them, treat them or, in the worst cases, put them down? There will always be those willing to try their luck because the rewards are so great, just as they are for the boatmen who transport thousands of illegal immigrants from northern Africa in equally desperate conditions in search of a better life in Italy and further into Europe. The difference, of course, is that the illegal immigrants have a choice and for those who make it there is a possibility of a better life. If the horses and ponies survive their journey, all that awaits them is the butcher's knife.

It is a question of priorities for the politicians who pass the laws and who should see that they are being enforced. Worrying about the fate of a lorry load of horses and ponies does not seem to register with many authorities and, worse, they are prepared to turn a blind eye to the problem. There can be no other explanation. Why else would this illegal transportation be allowed to continue? Every country through which the lorries pass must know it is happening, so surely it would be easy enough to turn them back at the border?

Unless people are prepared to 'Make a Noise', as one of the WHW campaigns urges, the trade will continue. Until people stop trying to buy a horse or pony on the cheap because they like the idea of having a horse without any of the knowledge required, people will go on breeding and selling, 'no questions asked'. Every child is taught that it will get nothing for nothing and yet, as adults, we find it impossible to resist a bargain, even if that bargain Hanoverian was originally destined for the abattoir on account of some irreversible injury.

There is a passport system for horses – all are supposed to have one – but all too often it does not work or is abused. All horses and ponies coming through WHW farms are micro-chipped but, as we have noted, there is no centralised, European-wide database which can track the many thousands criss-crossing our borders.

Education, as we have been discussing, is the key in places like Africa or Central America, where the root cause of the abuse is poverty rather than wilful abuse or neglect. Their horses and donkeys are a lifeline to survival. They may also be a status symbol but are highly prized and sometimes even loved. In these countries it is ignorance of anything better, a lack of resources or even the absence of any medical or basic equine help which is the issue. If you know your horse should be shod and all you have available is a steel rod from a building site, then that is what you will use; somehow or other you will have to cope. Not for a moment is any harm meant.

The difference in these countries is that the students taught by WHW and other charities are more than eager to learn because for them it is, first and foremost, the opportunity for a new career. The most successful of them want to share their knowledge because they, too, value and care for horses and, like a benevolent virus, the word of good animal husbandry quickly spreads. In one sense it is easy to get our message across in the developing world where horse owners are desperate to learn how to look after their horses and ponies in a better way, because so much depends on the fitness of these animals, but it is clearly a different matter in places like Europe. I pin great hopes on the likes of the Pony

Club in Great Britain because it is reaching the very young and hopefully instilling into them the correct way to look after their ponies, a lesson which they can carry into adulthood. Great emphasis is now placed on teaching the members about the welfare of their ponies, the importance of the correct feed, shoeing and exercise as well, of course, as basic and advanced riding techniques as they progress through their tests.

But while the Pony Club may be teaching the correct methods of care, the message is clearly not always getting through elsewhere, as the endless calls to the WHW support lines testify.

Sadly, as the study into horse health and welfare by the University of Dublin showed, education also has to reach into areas like Ireland where horses are supposedly highly regarded. I wonder how much has changed since 2010, when the behaviour of horse owners, dealers, keepers at unregulated gatherings and those disposing of horses was regarded as critically unacceptable. There is no comprehensive identification system for horses, the traveller community remains impenetrable and the falling value of horses means our concerns should remain high. The report concluded that there was 'a need for a single comprehensive conduit of science-based information, education and training on horse health and welfare for the equine industries,' but nothing remotely comprehensive has emerged.

So where should we focus our attention and our efforts? In the developing world, it is a question of education, explaining to owners how they improve their care of their horses and donkeys. They need to be trained in the rudiments of farriery and harness making and, as a bonus where possible, nutrition, but that strikes me as almost a luxury in some regions of the world where there is not even enough food for families to eat.

In the developed world, a combination of education and stricter law enforcement is called for. The aim would be to increase awareness among people who may not have any intention of ever owning a horse, so they become alert to potential areas of neglect. Law enforcement not only has to be carried through, but should also be speeded up. It cannot be right that horses and ponies have to be left suffering while WHW and other charities wishing to help are obstructed by what amounts to legal chicanery, designed to delay due process.

Then – in what might be called the hinterland between developing and developed countries, such as some Eastern European nations – we must impose civilised standards of care. Just because horses have been treated in a particular way for years does not make it acceptable. I am pointing the finger here at the likes of Romania, where animals are starved, left in agony with untreated hooves or obscenely fattened for slaughter, some not even able to bear the weight of their own bodies. This has nothing to do with being an impoverished country. It is an attitude of mind which finds it acceptable to inflict suffering on helpless animals for profit. We should never forget, though, that the profit emerges only at the end of intolerably long, painful and unnecessary journeys. The real blame, therefore, lies with those countries – Italy in particular – which insist on receiving live horses into their abattoirs. Surely we must try and put pressure on the Italians to introduce legislation to bring this to an end?

12 | WHERE ARE WE NOW?

It only takes a moment on the internet to find a horse. Advertisements range from the perfectly reputable to the obviously dodgy: 'Free delivery – must go by the end of the week.' At this end, the seller has no interest in the buyer's ability to care for the horse, so long as he can get rid of it.

In 2012 horse charities were warning of a crisis; three years on, matters are worse. There are two fundamental reasons: indiscriminate breeding and the cost of upkeep. It costs on average £5,000– £6,000 a year to keep a horse for general use, as opposed to professional competition. Feed, tack, vet and farrier bills quickly add up and despite some signs of an economic upturn, the average home is still feeling the pinch and the luxuries are the first to go.

Low to average quality horses, though, have no value. As we have seen, a Dartmoor pony can be picked up for a fiver, so there is no guarantee that a ready buyer will be found even for a pony which has been well looked after, whose rider has simply outgrown it. What should the owners do? Horses can live to a great age. Their feet will still need trimming every six weeks, even if they are just left out in a field, and they will need occasional visits from the vet, for vaccinations, worming or some other mundane treatment. In the winter months horses need some form of shelter if they are living out, and it doesn't take long for a field to turn to mud after a few days of rain, which in turn can lead to infections such as mud fever. Anyone buying a horse or pony is taking on a commitment with possible long-term consequences and WHW advises people to think hard before taking on such a responsibility.

If people have no luck finding a buyer, many simply abandon their horses and ponies, leaving them to fend for themselves on the side of the road and, in the worst cases, to starve. It is not uncommon for animal welfare officers to find horses which have been tethered, lame from their shackles or even strangled to death by their head collars. Literally hundreds of horses and ponies are abandoned in the UK every year.

There are some 3,000 horses and ponies in farms run by the various welfare charities including WHW, but there must be at least double that number in need of rescue. This is a crisis which cannot be left to the charities themselves. There is no more room in our stables. It requires immediate intervention by government and local authorities. Private horse ownership is largely unregulated and a primary cause of the problem is irresponsible dealers who continue to import and breed in an already overcrowded market. This oversupply quickly leads to more abandoned horses and an increase in fly-grazing. Wales used to be the epicentre but, as tougher laws have been introduced there, more incidents can be found in small pockets from the Thames Estuary and the Midlands up to Yorkshire. In 2014, for instance, WHW noted about 1,000 more horses fly-grazing in England than in the year before. Less rigorous legislation, in other words, leads to more fly-grazing.

Increasingly, WHW farms are taking in batches of horses rather than individuals, which is a reflection of over-breeding as well as economic pressures. These horses and ponies are often unhandled, even wild, which means that special pens are required when they are unloaded so that they can be sorted and separated, micro-chipped and treated safely.

In the developing world, charities like WHW find it difficult to capture the attention of the heavy hitters in government when it comes to distributing development aid, and struggle to get the message across that working equids have a part to play.

Tom Morrison, a WHW trustee who has consulted on aid projects around the globe for 40 years, came up with a neat phrase when speaking at the 2014 WHW Colloquium on Working Equids, which was trying to decide where to put its backing. 'Follow the donkey,' he said. Three quarters of global poverty is rural and most equids are part of rural livelihoods. To follow the donkeys and the mules will always take you to where aid is needed. Put it another way: what would we do with all the aid parcels if there were no horses, donkeys and mules to deliver them?

The challenge, Tom felt, was to find a link between the targets for development aid and working equids, which were still operating in parallel but not in unity. He believed that the link between equine welfare and wider international development aid is a logical and strong one. Equine non-governmental organisations need to play a stronger role, working with major development agencies in directing aid, with the understanding that partnerships and matched funding are longer lasting and are much more sustainable than straight donations.

Encouragingly, coming as it does from a man with great knowledge of delivering aid in the most efficient manner, Tom believes that 'animal welfare is gradually being recognised as highly relevant in alleviating poverty.' He nevertheless points out that while every government has a programme to help its citizens, none has one to help its equids; Romania, which we have looked at elsewhere, even went so far at one stage as to ban horses from using made-up roads, which I can only assume was out of embarrassment. It is clearly important to establish the principle that helping working equids is beneficial to the recipient country as well as to the donor nations. A sound horse is a guarantee for a family that they will be able to earn a living and provide for all, including the horse; if families are healthy, so too is the community which begins to prosper and, ultimately, no longer depends on aid.

WHW takes precisely this approach. It is an holistic one, seeking to help not just the equids but, by keeping the animals healthy, allowing whole communities to thrive. It is adapting the charity's methodologies to suit the country rather than trying to bring in a ready-made answer, which is as bad as offering a new shoe for a horse regardless of the shape or condition of its hoof. When teachers teach, they must also learn from their students. If no one can afford expensive steel nippers, then adapt and use the locally-available knives to trim the horse's feet, but also teach the student how to shape the foot and how effective it is. It is a two-way process.

While I was chairman of WHW, we were already beginning to get a good handle on that fact, and I know that nothing is ever done in a country without thorough research in advance, often with the aid of university students. We quickly recognised the importance of affiliating with influential international bodies, such as the FEI, to make our voice heard. While there is obviously some way to go in moving the valuable contribution of working equids up the agenda both with national governments and aid donors, at least it is no longer considered an outlandish thought. If a family is on the receiving end of a Red Cross parcel delivered by a donkey which has trekked over the ruins of an earthquake to reach them, they are not going to complain about the method of delivery.

So it is imperative that human aid and animal welfare agencies work more closely together. In truth, human aid is catching up with the likes of WHW, The Brooke, SPANA and The Donkey Sanctuary, which were probably 20 years ahead of other charities in recognising the important link between animal and human aid. During the Darfur genocide in Western Sudan which began in 2003, it was noted that as the aid agencies moved in with their help, they raced past starving donkeys and mules, which could have been a huge help in the rescue mission. Those donkeys and mules were invisible to the NGOs, though, in their headlong rush to deliver aid. Why, in 2015, are we still talking about the need to seek closer collaboration? As it is, the starving, abandoned donkey walking across the camera shot is barely noticed when news crews record the latest tragedy for their 24-hour bulletins. This is not a plea to be nice to donkeys: this is a reminder that donkeys, mules and horses have a valuable role to play in any overall rescue plan and that when the fighting or the earthquakes or the floods are over, they will once again be essential for the recovery of the local economy.

It is the WHW view that working in close collaboration with human development is where it will have the biggest breakthrough. While significant sums of money are spent on development aid, none is going into equine needs. Agricultural animals – cows and goats – are recognised as part of the development mix but equines – horses, donkeys and mules, the vital part of everyday life in developing countries – remain invisible. It is a waste of a powerful resource and it makes no sense.

By contrast, we clearly have a long way to go in the 'developed' world when it comes to the treatment of horses, whether for entertainment or for food.

The law, my subject, has all the tools to bring to an end the long-distance transportation of horses for meat. The legislation is in place, but what is the point if it can be ignored with impunity? A horse owner in Honduras will change the way he treats his horse because he depends on it for his existence. A horse dealer in Romania knows there will always be another horse ready to be loaded into his lorry because there is money in it. It does not matter one jot to him what state the horse is in: it has a value, slightly higher alive than dead.

There seems to be a disconnect in government as aid is handed out to developing countries without a clear understanding of where it is required and used and, critically, of how it reaches those in most need. Officials are now gradually recognising the importance of improving the health of working equids and those same governments, which pass laws to prevent cruelty to horses on their doorstep, must spare the time and resources to enforce those laws and reward those seen to be promoting this approach.

I have spoken a great deal about donkeys, as well as horses and ponies, in this book. They are all equines and they all face varying degrees of hardship, not only in the UK but around the world. The four main international charities – WHW, The Brooke, SPANA and The Donkey Sanctuary – now meet together every six months to pool their knowledge and experience.

The Donkey Sanctuary was founded in 1969 by Dr Elisabeth Svendsen MBE and has been operating internationally for more than 30 years. Although donkeys may be linked in our minds with Africa and the Middle East, there are about 30,000 in the UK and, because they are bred for harsher, dustier and drier climates, they suffer similar problems to horses, such as overfeeding and laminitis. They are, though, quite different in their make-up and it is only in recent years that veterinary students have been taught about those important differences which mean that a donkey is not just another type of horse! Unlike horses, which respond to danger with either 'fight or flight', donkeys stand still when threatened – there is no point trying to outrun a predator in the desert. This also means that donkeys and mules are good at masking pain as well as fear.

Around the world there are estimated to be 50 million donkeys and mules, most of them working animals. By 2018, The Donkey Sanctuary hopes to have reached two million of them in more than 20 countries with the aim of delivering the Five Freedoms of the Brambell Report (1965) for the livestock husbandry:

- Freedom from hunger or thirst by ready access to fresh water and a diet to maintain full health and vigour
- Freedom from discomfort by providing an appropriate environment including shelter and a comfortable resting area
- Freedom from pain, injury or disease by prevention or rapid diagnosis and treatment
- Freedom to express (most) normal behaviour by providing sufficient space, proper facilities and company of the animal's own kind
- Freedom from fear and distress by ensuring conditions and treatment which avoid mental suffering.

It does not seem to be asking a lot of their owners.

Just like WHW, the focus of The Donkey Sanctuary around the world is as much to educate owners as to treat donkeys in pain. Sometimes it takes very little to make a huge difference. Kevin Brown, International Programme Development Manager, said that at one brickyard they were able to demonstrate that by halving the load a donkey was made to carry back and forth to the kilns, it could actually work faster and therefore carry more bricks in its working day than if weighed down. It resulted in a happier donkey and a more productive brickyard.

David Cook, Chief Executive of The Donkey Sanctuary, says the fate of donkeys is sometimes to end up in the food chain. Just like horse meat, this is an issue that has to be faced. He notes that most of the donkeys in China look well cared for, because they tend to be worked until they are seven or eight and are then slaughtered for food. Given that donkeys can live into their thirties, the question is: which is better? A short and happier life or a prolonged life of possible suffering and neglect? There are no easy answers but it is a debate that everyone who cares for these animals should enter.

What are we to make of individuals in Great Britain who choose to mistreat horses, ponies and donkeys simply because no one seems to care? Once again, laws are in place but the punishments may not fit the crime: a ban on keeping horses for a few months is easily circumvented by another member of the family and not even a short prison sentence deters the guilty. It requires something tougher, as proved by the instant reaction of people fly-grazing their horses when faced with tough-looking bailiffs: they swiftly move on to new 'pastures'. It seems to me that the fly-grazing problem would be resolved within a year if every council adopted similar uncompromising measures. It would be a start if the same law were applied across England, Scotland and Wales.

The people who abuse animals in this way are cowards. They do what they do because no one stops them and because the unfortunate horses uncomplainingly allow themselves to be mistreated in this way. It may be the tradition of traveller groups to own horses, but when youngsters hammer immature horses up and down the roads as 'part of their training' without knowledge or understanding of the physical wellbeing of the horses and ponies, should they be allowed to keep them? Travellers no longer 'travel' as they used to and much of any historical, innate knowledge of how to care for horses has been lost. 'We have our rights!' will be the response to that, but where is the voice of the horse? It, too, has rights.

I started this book talking about the sports horse which could be described as the top of the pyramid. Princess Haya, speaking from a background in Olympic riding, said at the 2014 Colloquium on Working Equids that sports horses protect the concept of welfare and provide a platform from which to celebrate working horses. 'I have seen how elite sport horses are greatly valued, while the working horse is almost invisible, despite their value to the livelihoods of many poorer countries. In most cases the people who depend on working equines do not have a voice and generally do not receive any assistance apart from that provided through development organisations. To these people, their horse, donkey, or mule may be the single most important thing in ensuring their livelihoods. It therefore seems natural that those working in human development and those in animal welfare should be working together to the same end.

'For example, a man in Phnom Penh uses his pony for collecting building materials and the income from that to feed his family. This pony is as important to him as a competition horse is to a rider competing in the Olympics. However, in equestrian sport, we recognise that for a horse to compete well its health, fitness and well-being is of paramount importance. To ensure this, in many countries, we have access to a whole industry of skilled farriers, saddlers and vets. Working horses, ponies, donkeys and mules also need this care – but their needs are often unmet because of a lack of awareness of what their horses need, and a lack of skilled people to provide these services.'

Sadly, there is a new threat within the equine sports industry and it doesn't come from drugs or cheating: it stems from a change in attitudes. The concept of winning fair and square, having enjoyed the challenge, has often been replaced with an attitude of 'win at all costs'. It seems to be the winning that matters; so long as a competitor can stand on the podium holding the trophy, he is happy, and how that 'victory' was achieved, no matter how hollow it might be, is of no consequence. I wonder what goes through the mind of such a person, who knows that the win was only possible because of surreptitious means: anabolic steroids administered in the privacy of a stable or a quick injection behind the sand dunes as a 'booster' in one of those tough endurance events. Can that individual ever be considered a sportsman? And what of the horses that have been abused in this way? How many are simply cast aside, their bodies ruined by abuse, having delivered that tarnished trophy? I have heard that the figure runs into the hundreds, maybe more.

When the sprinter Tyson Gay returned to athletics in Lausanne in July 2014 after serving a one-year doping ban, his colleague, Justin Gatlin, who had also been caught, warned that the cloud hanging over every future performance would never go away. He said: 'It is going to be a stressful time not only on the track but what the media thinks about you, what people think about you and how they look at you. It's probably going to be with him for the rest of his career. (*Daily Telegraph*, 3 July 2014). Come the race, the 100 metres at the Diamond League meeting, Gatlin won, Gay was second and Mike Rodgers, who had also served a doping ban, was third. The headline in the paper next day read: 'Gatlin wins battle of the drug cheats'. (*Daily Telegraph*, 4 July 2014)

That same year, the World Cup attracted suspicions over match-fixing and, in cricket, Lou Vincent, the New Zealand player who was banned for life after pleading guilty to 18 breaches of anti-corruption regulations, admitted that he had been tempted by greed: 'I thought: 'Yeah, I'm going to make some big money now, so stuff the world.' (*Daily Telegraph*, 3 July 2014).

Recognizing that science is constantly changing, Sir Craig Reedie, president of the World Anti-Doping Agency, said that the agency would consider even longer bans for athletes who fail dope tests if it could be proved that performance-enhancing substances had longer term benefits (*Daily Telegraph*, 28 October 2014). Clearly there is no point in banning athletes for just two or four years if their muscles retain the advantages of anabolic steroids after the ban is lifted.

I see the 'must win' attitude in racing, I see it in eventing and I see that 'me first' approach even in junior and Pony Club riding. At the risk of sounding old fashioned and out of touch, there was a time when every member of a family which kept one or more horses would know and care about them; it would be in the genes. Today, if one can afford a horse, why not have several? So much the better if they turn out to be winners. Don't expect, though, that the new breed of owners with no background in horses will help out at a show, sit all day in the pouring rain as a jump judge or stand at the collecting ring while dozens of young riders enjoy their few minutes on the course before packing up and heading home. Equally, don't expect every horse owner to have any sort of genuine affection for their animals. If the pony doesn't suit, so the thinking seems to go, it can just be shifted off to a dealer's unwelcoming yard to make room for another – a prettier, faster, bigger one – without a second thought for the real feelings of the pony, which may finally have settled after being moved from pillar to post. Some people do not deserve to own horses. I generalise, of course, but the attitude is prevalent and offers a poor prospect for the future.

The world is so small now. It is no use bemoaning the passing of 'standards'. Racing is an international sport and what was once championed by the Jockey Club, and is now managed by the BHA, seems to count for little. We in Britain can no longer say: 'If you want to join our party, you must play by our rules,' because we no longer have enough clout or, to be vulgar about it, enough money. The big cash prizes in sport are to be found away from the British Isles. Illegal gambling is now a multi-trillion dollar enterprise being driven by dealers from the Far East and they are affecting every level of sport, fixing football matches, bribing officials and nobbling runners and riders.

Back in 2008, WHW carried a report in its magazine by Graham Capper, senior enforcement officer for Trading Standards, in which he concluded, after a three-year study into the state of equine welfare in Wales, that irresponsibility, ignorance and greed were rife. He suspected that similar problems would be found throughout the country. It is clear that greed, at least, is still rampant in many sports, not just in Great Britain but worldwide.

So what should be done about it? Tougher policing, tougher penalties? Maybe, but there is a clear reluctance to hand down lifetime bans for offenders. Should we care if an athlete is getting stronger and faster because of steroids? Why not let them all do it and judge them on their ability to master the science of the laboratory as much as their dedication to training? If a runner or, for that matter, a race horse returns after a suspension for steroid abuse, it is impossible to say what residual benefit is contributing to performance. The discussion about Lasix continues.

The problem is that soon we will never be able to trust the results. We may even have already passed that point. By 2014 it had become difficult to watch cycling, football, cricket, athletics or horse racing without sometimes wondering about the honesty of the result. And everyone was being tarred with the same brush. If even great horse trainers like Martin Pipe, who worked meticulously with their horses, carefully monitoring their feeds, constantly taking their temperatures, timing every run and even recording daily rainfall levels, delivered a string of winners, people would ask suspiciously: 'How did he do it?' He, like many others in the sport, did it honestly, through dedication over long years, but others want to take the fast track to success and sometimes achieve it just because they are prepared to pay any price to be the winner. Incidentally, who other than Martin Pipe would hang blown-up photographs of trees and grass in the stables to make them look more natural and install skylights to let in more daylight to help calm their horses?

To be a winner in Choluteca, Mexico is to bring in $15 dollars a day to feed the family and have a little left over to feed and care for the horse. To be a winner in Soweto is to toil long hours hauling waste to rubbish dumps, knowing that your pony will have the strength in his aching limbs to do it all over again the next day. To be a winner in Ethiopia is to be a mother with a healthy donkey which can fetch the water every day for her family so that she can cook and wash without having to make the backbreaking journey to the river herself.

WHW has helped countless thousands of these people become winners in this way, thanks to the generosity of many supporters. There are probably 100 million working equids around the world and it is safe to say that the majority need some sort of help to improve their lives and to enable their owners, in many cases, to survive. This is the alternative face of the equine world. It demands our attention because it increases prosperity in countries which, despite their hardships, are rapidly expanding.

Why bother helping? Even if we don't care about the horses and donkeys it makes economic sense to help. The population of Africa will more than double to 2.4 billion over the next 40 years, according to the Population Reference Bureau of America, and economic growth in sub-Saharan Africa is forecast to increase to 6.1 per cent in 2014–2015 (*Recycling our Future – A Global Strategy* by Ranjit S.Baxi, Whittles Publishing). Areas like Africa have to be helped to achieve the same prosperity as the rest of the world precisely because it is beneficial to the rest of the world. And if most of the African population is living in rural communities dependent on donkeys and mules just to get through the day, it is logical that those animals should be nurtured and protected. It is, as Tom Morrison, says: a win/win situation.

So what is going to happen next? In the harsh reality of the developing world, equines of all sorts will continue to labour long hours in appalling conditions, and all the rest of us can do is be aware of the important role they play in their owners' everyday lives. To recognise that they are a vital cog in any relief effort and must therefore be protected will at least be a first step.

In a country like England, the idyllic scene of Suffolk Punches ploughing the fields, guided by a farmer who knew precisely what he had to do to look after his working horse, may now be the stuff of history and faded paintings; that knowledge is no longer bred into people. Even the racing yards of old would have had far fewer horses and probably more stable hands to look after them. Everyone was more involved, it seems to me, and I fear so much basic training has been lost. Working in a yard is no longer a passion: it's just another way of escaping from the dole. Some trainers are good at educating their staff, while others may hardly bother at all, probably because they know the lads will not last the distance. And if there are a hundred or more horses in the yard, there is simply no time to teach as well as train. The duty of the head lad in any stable is to pass on his knowledge and teach those working in the stable. A lad who worked for me, who rode well and went on to a racing yard, said he was never given any instruction when he got there; they just put him on one of the horses and got him to ride out. It was such a pity because he had talent and the desire to progress.

Economics is another key factor. Very few racing trainers in the UK make serious money. Their horses have to travel hundreds of miles to take part in races all over the country and sometimes on the continent, there is much more paperwork to be completed than there used to be, and average prize money at minor weekday meetings is low, starting at around £2,500 and possibly going up to £10,000 which would be a big win.

There are some cheery stories amidst all the gloom, though. Aidan O'Brien, champion trainer of horses racing on the flat in Ireland, including the 2014 Derby winner, Australia, told me he was not a good sleeper because he was constantly worrying about his horses. If he wakes up in the middle of the night, he said, he may well go outside in his dressing gown, and if he sees a horse needing hay, he will fetch it himself. That is passion, as far removed from doping and abuse as it is possible to get, but the point is that the best trainers are hands on. Many have ridden themselves and, so long as the money is there, they will always put their horses first.

The intuitive instinct of what is right for a horse was clearly in the O'Brien genes. Once, when we were at Ballydoyle, we were invited to watch some of his young horses in a gallop. Several top jockeys were riding, as well as Aidan's young son, Joseph, and each wore a headset. Aidan thus controlled their speed. Following the gallop all the jockeys returned on foot to be asked their opinions of the horses' work that morning. When it came to young Joseph's turn he replied: 'I think the filly thinks she's better than she really is.' This was May 2010. Joseph won the Epsom Derby in 2012 and has ridden many group winners for his father around the world.

However, time and again we have taken a horse from a trainer's yard and found that it won't come anywhere near the front of its box. This, I presume, is because it has been hit about by impatient stable lads or impatient jockeys tacking it up, cursing and swearing if it moves. Impatience with horses takes us back to the Pony Club and learning the basics of animal behaviour.

Cherry Michell, who retired as chairman of the Pony Club after six years in 2013, worries about the 'lost generation' of youngsters who have little or no experience of animals in general, let alone horses. 'You can no longer say that every child has patted a pony,' she said. 'Fifty or sixty years ago there was no reason why a child who wanted to have contact with a horse couldn't at that stage. But I think today, unfortunately, they are not part of everyday life any more than dogs are. The rag and bone man with his horse and cart would have been a familiar sight in towns and even in mining villages children would have seen the pit ponies when they came up from the mines for their summer holiday.

'It is the parents we are really worried about. I think our job is to educate the next generation of children because we can only do so much for this group of parents. What we are up against is not only do we have the children with non-horsey parents, but the generation who should now be volunteers are too busy earning the money so the child can have the pony.'

There are multiple targets to promote horse welfare. At the professional level, jockeys have to attend courses at Newmarket racing school if they want to ride in races under rules. In the past, the trainers would have been much more involved in the education of their jockeys but today there is so much more racing, making it impractical for trainers to spare the time. They rely on hugely experienced head lads in this aspect. There are all-weather tracks and more courses ready to start racing and wanting fixtures, although I would say that it is ridiculous even to contemplate having any more racing in the UK, as numbers are already severely depleted, as acknowledged by the BHA. Paul Bittar, its Chief Executive, said that small field sizes were 'arguably the biggest challenge facing British racing in recent years.' (*Racing Post*, 22 October 2014). There is a course in Essex, Chelmsford City, which has opened and closed twice, but since coming under new ownership has now been granted 58 fixtures, enabling the owners to start racing again. It would suit the trainers in Newmarket to have an all-weather track nearer them rather than having to go over to Kempton, Lingfield or Southwell, but they are all chasing minimal prize money; by the time the owner has paid the jockey, trainer and transport there is not much left from a £2,500 win and nothing at all for those who lost.

Away from racing, in eventing, show jumping and endurance riding, the FEI seems to have its work cut out, given that it sets out to keep the welfare of the horse at the heart of all its activities. More and more cases of drug abuse, painfully thin endurance horses and outright cheating keep cropping up. This has nothing to do with a lack of tradition or of understanding about how to look after horses; it is about winning at all costs. When such cases are uncovered, everyone seems to nod wisely and say, 'Oh yes, we all knew that!' but why, then, does no one speak up? People question whether it is even ethical to use horses in sport. WHW certainly believes that it is perfectly ethical, but that all those involved have to demonstrate beyond a shadow of doubt that everything is being done for the welfare of the horse. As I have already shown, horses bred for racing love to race and, as Princess Haya says, investment in sports horses benefits the entire industry. But it is only by maintaining a constant scrutiny on such matters as the use of the whip, the construction of jumps and the stresses involved in endurance competition that those of us who love equine sports will be able to carry the sceptics with us.

In the context of what should happen next, why is more not being done to stop the appalling long-distance transportation of horses to Italy, not just from Romania but also from Spain and Portugal? Thanks to the pressure from the likes of WHW, as we have noted, there cannot be a politician in Europe who is unaware of the problem. None, though, is willing to apply effective pressure on the Italians to change their ways. To push horse welfare up the political agenda is a hard task, but not one that is going to be shirked. It was once acceptable to smoke in public places, but eventually that was changed. Eating horse meat is not going to do anyone any harm, but who can really tell the difference between salami prepared from horses which have endured long, tortuous hours in a lorry and salami prepared from horses that have been killed in their country of origin, frozen, then shipped?

Fortunately, welfare is a priority for many horse owners and so long as the likes of the Pony Club, the FEI, the British Show Jumping Association (BSJA), the British Horse Society (BHS) and the BHA continue to promote it, then change will come about. While mothers and fathers are prepared to pay for their children's ponies to be shod, to buy new tack and pay to enter local events, while people turn up in their thousands to watch events, dressage and show jumpers perform and while races such as the Oaks, the Derby and Grand National attract the public in sufficient numbers, then there is hope. Hope, because these people are the ones who can apply economic pressure – the only kind that counts these days – for equestrian sport to demonstrate that it is clean and, above all, caring towards the very creatures upon which these sportsmen and -women depend.

In the developing world there is also hope, thanks to the generosity of donors and sponsors coupled with the work of volunteer vets, farriers and saddlers who know that they are making a difference.

It is making a difference in places like Honduras, where working horses provide essential services to over 80% of the population. When just one training course in Choluteca transforms the quality of life for 145 horses by improving their harnesses and ensuring they are properly shod, it not only changes the lives of the horses, but improves the economic prospects for their owners and their families.

It makes a difference when WHW can use £100,000 in donations to support our teams in Haiti because now, for instance, nearly 400 horse owners have become aware of the training programmes, ensuring that 100 horses and donkeys which carry tourists to visit the sites can now do so without pain.

It has been making a difference in Senegal since 2008, when WHW began work to establish strong links with the government to help our teams of instructors reach right out into the more rural communities. Even in rapidly developing cities like the capital, Dakar, it is the horses and donkeys, carrying essential supplies, which are helping drive the economy from behind the scenes. Everyone can make a difference.

13 | OUR FARMS

World Horse Welfare operates four farms in the UK, providing rescue, rehabilitation and rehoming to the horses and ponies it takes in. They represent about a third of the charity's £7.5 million annual budget and are a significant and vital part of WHW's work, which continues in many different parts of the world. Hundreds of animals pass through their gates every year and it is difficult to see when the sad flow will come to an end. Every week the new influx presents WHW with difficult decisions; the harsh reality is that a horse may be too sick, too old, too lame or just too unmanageable ever to hope to find a new, caring home.

BELWADE, ABOYNE, SCOTLAND

To respond to the daily calls for help throughout Scotland, including the islands of Orkney and the Hebrides, Belwade depends on just three field officers. Doug Howie covers east of Stirling, Angus, Aberdeenshire, Moray and Shetland, Jim Maxwell is responsible for everything further west, including the Hebrides, while John Burns covers Central Scotland and the Borders. It is a large territory to monitor and even though the officers report cheerfully that they like to keep busy, I fear they are sitting on a welfare time bomb.

Scotland does not seem to have the fly-grazing problem so familiar to people living in the south but appearances are deceptive. While there is only a small traveller community north of the border, the remote hillsides conceal a darker problem. Eileen Gillen, Belwade Farm Manager for 25 years, says: 'The number we are saying 'no' to, outweighs the number we can take in. We can only take so many.'

When I visited the farm in August 2014 they had 79 horses and ponies, when the ideal maximum should have been 65. With long experience, Eileen is not one to pull her punches: 'Where do the horses come from? There are two ways of looking at it. It doesn't matter what walk of life they may be bred into, whether they are the hoarders or the good-lifers who have a lot of disposable income in Aberdeenshire, because the oil boom protected us from the recession. People start by getting a smallholding, they buy a few lambs, then the Muscovy ducks, then they get a couple of Shetland ponies and the holding gets bigger and bigger. They think they are doing good. But before they realise it, their smallholding is now an overgrown farm with big herds of ponies because what they don't do is castrate the young, entire ponies. That is definitely on the increase.

'On the other side you have got people who want to make money out of them but, in this case, the recession hasn't helped because the value of horses and ponies has plummeted and yet they haven't stopped breeding. They may well have started as good quality horses but as the neglect starts, they are no better off than the itinerant horses that keep coming in. Are they any different to the race horses which get thrown on the heap or the show jumper or the dressage horse?'

The Grampian region has a very high-density equine population, which surprises people. Where there is one Shetland pony, there are ten, twenty or more. Within a radius of 20 miles of Belwade were owners with 200 Shetland ponies, and another just ten miles away was one with about 300 ponies. While the ponies were being looked after there was less concern than there might have been, but the question, inevitably, was what would happen in the years ahead, when the owners were no longer around to look after them?

Then there are the cases when people simply tire of their horses or their children want to give up riding. They call the farm and ask if the charity will take them in. Eileen's response is usually: 'Give me ten reasons why we should take your horse. If you bought it or bred it, surely it is your responsibility to look after it?' On the other hand, there are cases of genuine concern, which is where the field officers come in, to try first to offer advice. Bringing horses and ponies to Belwade is always the last resort; the priority is to help the owners to keep their animals at home.

Doug Howie, a former mounted policeman, is slow to apportion blame. Neglect and cruelty are two totally different things, he says. Neglect creeps up on people slowly for different reasons; sometimes they don't even notice their horses losing weight. When there are financial problems in the family, the first thing to go is the feed. But he believes that it is seldom down to wilful or wanton neglect.

When neglect does happens, it often requires all the psychological training he acquired during his time in the force, first to win the trust of the offending owners, who may not even recognise the harm they are causing, and then to be able to move in quickly to rescue the animals.

Doug found a case where owner had simply piled up dead carcases in a barn or left them where they fell in the fields, rather than accept that the situation was out of control. The owners either chose to ignore the fate of these animals or, where they have been hidden away in a barn, they know precisely what they are doing and will do anything not to be caught out. These are extreme and dreadful cases which upset even the most hardened of field officers but as herds grow, as they are doing, welfare issues will become more frequent.

A tip he offers any would-be horse owner is to remember that horses like routine whether for exercise or feeding. Break it at your peril. He remembers one day in particular while out on patrol:

'When I was in the police we used to go out at 9 a.m. and come back two and a-half hours later. The horses used to know where they were and when they were about ten minutes from the stable. So you almost accommodated their routine.

'On one occasion, one of my colleagues, John, was in George Square in Glasgow and thought he had to make up a bit of time so he let his horse have a wee trot. It happened to be a strong-willed horse. He headed off down Queen Street which meets Argyle Street at a right angle. As he was half way down Queen Street the horse, Culruss, thought, 'I can have a wee canter here!' John decided it was making up time nicely so just let him canter. The next thing he knew he was galloping flat out down Queen Street. There were cars trying to get out of the way. At the bottom he had to make a right turn just in front of a shop.

'The studs on the shoes of the horse worked well on the road but when John overshot the turning onto the pavement flagstones there was no grip and the horse went straight forward. Thankfully it was the summer and the doors of a department store in front of them were open as Culruss went straight through the space about 12 feet, through another set of doors, down three steps and managed to stop at the cosmetics counter.

'John tried to get the horse back up the steps but it wouldn't move. He put out a coded message – Code 21, calling for assistance. I rushed down, I was on horseback, and I could see the marks on the road. I could see where he trotted, I could see where he cantered and galloped. I was on the radio saying: 'Where are you?' On the corner there was a drunk who said: 'Your mate's in there,' pointing down into the shop. I got someone to hold my horse and went in. John could not get his horse to shift. Then I noticed on the cosmetic counter there were some sample bottles of perfume. It was the men's counter and there was a tin of deodorant. So I lifted the horse's tail, gave him a spray and he shot up the stairs out through the door faster than he came down. Perhaps not perfect horse welfare, but he smelt better than when he came in.'

It is very easy to buy a horse but by buying it, you make a commitment. Belwade made a commitment. The facilities, including a spectacular indoor school and visitors' reception area, theatre and restaurant, make it a remarkable tourist attraction. At its core, though, is the message that horses and ponies need protection, sometimes from ourselves.

The familiar twin enemies are laminitis and ragwort. Laminitis is extremely painful and after a horse has suffered from it once, it is susceptible to suffering again, even on only a small patch of grass.

Ragwort is a nationwide problem. Landowners can be prosecuted if their fields are allowed to become overgrown with it, but very often it is local authorities who seem blind to the bright yellow flower growing at the side of the road, its seeds blowing on the wind to adjacent fields.

In short, then, it is all about education. Belwade is a mine of equine education, from the sometimes harrowing films on show in the lecture theatre there, which illustrate the tough work carried out day in, day out by WHW staff, to the advice they give to all horse owners who only need to ask. Like the other farms, it works closely with universities and veterinary bodies, pooling their different experience to help prevent equine disease; at Belwade, the wide variety of horses passing through the farm provides invaluable data for the Royal Dick School of Veterinary Studies in Edinburgh.

Each horse or pony at the farm costs £5,000– £6,000 a year to keep, including their feed, worming vet and farrier. From the time of getting the first phone call, it costs £200– £300 just to get the horse or pony to the farm, involving the time and effort of the field officer, a transportation vet, vaccinations and blood tests. The average stay before rehoming is nine months, which is quite short if one considers that they may be dealing with a pony which has never been handled.

For a horse-loving operation, their top priority may sound odd: they want to educate people away from getting a horse in the first place, because very often they have not given any thought to what they will do with that horse in the future. The first question everyone should ask is: do I really need a horse?

PENNY FARM, BLACKPOOL

'Unfortunately, being involved with horses doesn't necessarily mean you love horses.' This sad but perceptive observation by Penny Thornton, the benefactor who helped create the centre that was named after her, explains precisely why there is a need for charities like WHW.

There should be 65 horses and ponies at Penny Farm, but more often than not there are up to 80. When the centre was formally opened in 2001 by HRH The Princess Royal, the official capacity was 55, and it has grown steadily ever since. There are new stable blocks, an isolation wing, barns, paddocks and riding arenas. As Fran Williamson, the farm manager, says: 'The problem is not going to go away, so the key thing is to manage it by deciding what we bring in and what we don't.' And as they know that every time they turn a horse away, its suffering is only prolonged, the centre has an almost elastic capacity as the staff juggle the accommodation and work longer hours, particularly in the winter months when the service they provide is in greatest demand.

Penny Thornton, a former Trustee, has long been interested in horse welfare, particularly in the plight of working horses and donkeys overseas, where there is not the option of giving a horse six months' box rest to recover from injury because it has to be back in harness within half a day. In some countries the reality is that owners have to have a completely different outlook towards their horses, it doesn't mean they don't care.

Penny realised that, although the charity had a number of centres, there was a large tract of territory across the UK between Norfolk and Scotland, including the Isle of Man, which had no cover. She offered to get involved, as she modestly puts it, and after much research settled on an old dairy near Blackpool which was up for auction. It had good motorway links and was also handily placed near a major tourist resort, to attract visitors with time on their hands.

Eventually, Tony Fleming, ex-King's Troop, became the first farm manager and the centre is now firmly established, thanks to the help of the first volunteers like Zoe Clifford, the visitors' manager, who came on a part-time basis and never left, and field officers like Chris Williamson, Fran's husband, and John Cunningham, all ex-mounted police officers. Like the other WHW bases, it rescues, rehabilitates and rehomes, and also places a major emphasis on education.

As Fran will tell visitors, many people are misguided rather than wilfully negligent. They might say that they have bought a pony for £5, believing that they have 'saved' it, and yet they have no idea how to care for it or how much that care is going to cost. A common story is that parents say that their daughter is seven, she has had a few riding lessons and now would like to buy a pony. When they are asked who would look after the pony: 'Oh, she will!' Seven-year-old children cannot look after ponies; it is far better to go on having riding lessons at a yard. Unfortunately, more often than not, they go ahead and buy the pony and Penny Farm gets a knock on the door six months later.

Things may go well for a number of years, on the other hand, until eventually the child grows into a teenager and loses interest in riding or leaves home and goes to university. The parents are then left with a horse which they have no idea how to care for and, inevitably, it becomes neglected. There is no point taking the case to court, so the best solution is to get the horse signed over to WHW and quickly removed to safety. It is another mouth to feed and another horse to rehome if possible, but the alternative is worse.

This is what happens on a regular basis at centres like Penny Farm. They are not isolated cases and, sadly, when it comes to social welfare situations and a horse or pony is involved, the animal is last on the list of priorities and often poorly understood by police officers.

Chris, who spent 14 years as a field officer, said he used to carry a copy of the relevant Act of Parliament in order to explain the correct procedure to bemused police officers, who were probably being confronted by a horse for the first time. They were usually relieved to be able to sign the horse over.

More often than not it is the general public who are the eyes and ears of WHW and occasionally they go well beyond the call of duty. John Cunningham recalls a lady and her friend who took it upon themselves to help a group of horses in Accrington, East Lancashire.

The horses belonged to a local traveller who only met the animals' basic needs, leaving them tethered on rough ground. He failed to care for them but not badly enough to be prosecuted.

The two ladies would go out in all weathers to feed them, giving them extra hay and water. They also made sure the horses had dry, waterproof rugs when the conditions were really bad, swapping them at night and drying the rugs at home. They said that they did this, at their own expense, because they loved the horses. John likened them to the French Resistance in their stealth and determination, operating sometimes under cover of darkness to avoid being seen by the owner, who would hurl abuse if he caught them in the act.

John explained to the ladies that if WHW were to get anywhere with the case and prosecute the owner, they would have to stop their activities to allow the neglect to be confirmed. They could not bear to see the horses suffer and preferred to carry on doing what they were doing rather than resorting to the law. John said he admired the ladies' guts and determination: without making a song and dance about their actions, they cared for the horses in the face of abuse from the traveller, expecting no reward and without invoking Facebook. He warns others against following their example, though, as it might have adverse consequences.

Every region of the country has slightly different issues to contend with. Scotland seems to have the problem of much larger herds of animals, but in Penny Farm, in a more built-up area, they find ponies in back gardens. In the Bolton area there are horses everywhere, collecting scrap metal.

Occasionally, Penny Farm does have to take in big numbers. Their biggest case involved a farm in Cumbria, when WHW had to find room for 32 ponies. It is a story which illustrates both how matters can get out of hand without any deliberate intention to be cruel and also how the unreported skills of diplomacy, tact and patience play an important part in the life of a field officer.

It all began harmlessly enough when a man bought a Shetland pony for his daughter. Then he bought another one and then another one, allowing them to run free on the fells. In time, with no control on the breeding, there were soon more than a hundred ponies. They were never malnourished, but with so many wild ponies, it was impossible to care for their feet or geld the young stallions.

Finally, the National Parks, who had been trying to get the owner to do something about the problem for years, said action needed to be taken and called in WHW and the RSPCA to help. Chris, the field officer in charge, remembers the owner as something of a character. Before new licensing laws had been brought in, he used to keep two lions on his farm, which he would play with in their cage. The day before inspectors arrived he decided to clean out the cage, but one of the lions smelled something on his clothes and attacked him. He managed to get out by covering himself with an upturned wheelbarrow; his shirt was ripped to shreds and he was covered in cuts and scratches. The next day, dressed to cover up the cuts, he went back into the cage to prove to the inspectors that the lions were safe, but the regulations had changed and, as he did not have a licence to keep wild animals, the RSPCA had no choice but to remove his 'pets'. He later had another issue with an RSPCA inspector, went to court, defended himself and got off. He even hit a policeman who came onto his property and still won the day.

Suffice it to say that he had a burning hatred of the RSPCA and all authority, so when the time came to tackling the hundreds of ponies roaming the fells, Chris knew 'it would be war'. The problem would require great sensitivity and when he visited the farm, he and the owner talked about everything other than the horses, leaning on a fence as though passing the time of day. Eventually the owner relaxed and invited Chris into the house for a cup of coffee, where he explained that he would have to return to help the owner with the ponies. He duly did, accompanied by an RSPCA inspector. The owner said Chris could come in but the inspector would have to wait outside. Eventually he relented and allowed the inspector in, on condition that he didn't say a word.

In the end a vet was brought in from outside and produced a damning report. When the owner read it, he feared that all the ponies would be taken away, just like the lions. And that is exactly what happened.

Chris said: 'They turned up with all these round pens. I was called out but I was not allowed to speak to him and he was taken to the police station. They took all the horses. Redwings, RSPCA and the BHS took some, and 32 came to Penny Farm. When they arrived they were totally feral, some even had to be sedated to put a head collar on.

'When he was released from custody and got home, he said to his daughter that he needed to go out for a drive on the fells. She wouldn't let him go on his own, but when they called in at a petrol station and she went to pay, he drove off. He drove straight to the churchyard and hanged himself.'

After the funeral, the family asked to come and see the ponies that WHW had taken in. They were shown round and were told what WHW did and how we did it. They asked to keep a small group of about five, which they were allowed to do after making improvements to the stabling. The man's widow and daughter later invited Chris to their farm, saying: 'You are very welcome here any time and we will deal with you.' One day they came to Penny Farm and gave Chris a copy of a book the man had written about his life story, which his family had published after his death.

Everyone who works at WHW centres has this same enormous capacity for patience and understanding. Although the Cumbria story ended in tragedy for the family, it shows, I hope, that it is possible to make a difference and to help people understand. It takes time, though, because the owners, more often than not, have as many welfare issues as the horses and ponies.

A footnote to that story is that 13 of the mares that came to Penny Farm were in foal, meaning that the youngsters at least had a good start in life, even if they did increase the farm's numbers rather rapidly.

It is, above all, the equine characters which attract visitors to the centres. Dale, the Shetland pony, is the Penny Farm mascot, while probably the most famous resident was Penny, named after Penny Thornton, who arrived at the farm miserable and flea-bitten, cowering in the corner of her stable. One of the girls would sit on a stool by her stable with a bucket of feed. Every ten minutes or so, Penny would come out and take a mouthful of feed, then scuttle back. She had had no contact with people at all but the late Tony Fleming, former manager of Penny Farm and a member of the King's Troop Royal Horse Artillery, saw potential and said that, one day, she would be a troop horse. He was right.

She joined the army where her job was part of the gun team pulling one of the six World War I guns under her official name, Hallmark. Her position was 'on the wheel' where her chunky build helped her act as a brake horse. She was involved in many of the big parades; the first was the Queen Mother's funeral, then every Queen's birthday parade, the Jubilee celebrations, Prince Charles' and the Duke of Edinburgh's birthdays, the Lord Mayor of London's parade and, one of her last outings, to mark the birth of Prince George.

Just like all other rehomed horses, she returned to Penny Farm on her retirement for a formal handover by the Troop and a last display by Penny and her fellow horses. She is now enjoying a well-earned rest, rehomed with an ex King's Troop soldier, having been a great ambassadress for the work of WHW. Every year people came to see Penny, even though her manners left a little to be desired. After about half an hour greeting her 'fans', she would put her ears back as though she had had enough. King's Troop horses regularly come to Penny Farm for their holiday and make quite a spectacle, galloping along the beach in front of the Blackpool Tower, in and out of the sea.

The other annual event which keeps Penny Farm on its toes is the famous Appleby Horse Fair in June, when some 15,000 members of the traveller community from England, Ireland, Scotland and Wales descend on the tiny market town in Westmoreland, as they have been doing since the days of James II. In 1685 he granted a charter allowing a horse fair 'near the River Eden', where the purpose is to buy and sell horses with a traditional slap of the hand.

Most of the business is conducted on Long Marton Road, known as the 'flashing lane', where the horses and ponies show off – or 'flash' – their paces. In liaison with the RSPCA, field officers from WHW now set up stations, between the flashing lane and the river where the horses are washed off, to help with any injuries; vets are also there on a voluntary basis. There is a great deal of home-grown medication – one pony was being treated for a bad cut with a concoction of mustard. The vet cleaned off the wound, applied some cream and the owner was sent on his way. Payment is always at the discretion of the owner and vets consider themselves lucky if they get paid a couple of pounds for their services.

With extraordinary bonhomie, the staff of Penny Farm welcome hundreds of visitors every week, who may just drop in for one of the home-made cakes and a chat, or to see the latest intake of horses. The staff are always ready to educate the visitors and care for the residents because, until people learn the harsh facts about horse welfare, there will always be a sad and steady flow of ponies and horses through the gates.

GLENDA SPOONER FARM, SOMERSET

Glenda Spooner Farm can handle 65 horses and ponies and is only restricted to that number on its 200-acre site to ensure that there are enough grooms to care for the horses. The tragedy is that the field officers know they could fill the entire farm in a day with neglected and abandoned stock, even though the farm is managing to rehome home 8 –10 horses and ponies every month; the turnover of animals, to put it in brutal, commercial terms, is shocking.

Field officer Phil Jones, said: 'I have been doing this job for ten years and we are still only touching the tip of the iceberg. The main problem in the UK is indiscriminate breeding and the next problem is education. The horse is neither a pet nor a farm animal. It is classed as a companion animal. The Government brought in the passport and micro-chipping for traceability but it is a farce. With the farm animal you have traceability throughout its life but councils don't want to bother with horses because they don't have the money, the resources or the trained staff to deal with them. There is no point having a law if it is not enforced.'

As we have seen, indiscriminate breeding has driven down the price of the vast majority of horses and ponies. Claire Phillips, who has been the manager at the centre since 2011, believes there needs to be 'a huge cultural change across society which seems to have lost any sense of responsibility.' The finger is often pointed at the traveller community, but at what one might call the top end of equine sport there is also sharp practice. It is not uncommon for people to offer an ex-racehorse for sale at £400, including tack, 'from the field, no questions asked.' The unwitting buyers think they can just throw on a saddle and take it round a show jumping course, while in fact a racehorse needs to be professionally retrained. Without it, either the horse or the new owner will suffer.

With hundreds of horses and ponies waiting to be rescued, this is the 'tough love' which the UK has to wake up to as the equine crisis continues to develop. Some may think this is just a problem facing the fortunate few with money to spend on an expensive hobby, but the team at Glenda Spooner point out an unexpected fact: the number of horse owners on benefits is escalating. In one yard, the owner says 70% of her clients are on benefits. Another livery yard said most of her clients were on benefits, which she actually finds irritating because the clients used to come in for a ride and then go off to work – now, they hang around the yard all day because they have nothing else to do. Very often they are keeping more than one horse.

The common, and false, impression is that owning a horse means you have money to burn. In some communities, owning a horse increases your social standing; at one stage, dealers were going in to housing estates and giving horses away. One owner told Phil Jones that she had picked up a Shetland pony for just £80, taken it home, walked it straight through the house and put it in the garden. She very soon wanted to know what she should do with it next, though, because it had trashed the garden. They were feeding the pony straw and clearly had no idea how to look after the animal.

For field officers, it is not just a simple case of 'rescuing' the horse from such situations: there is a long list of economic, humanitarian and bureaucratic hurdles to jump first. Phil Jones explains: 'When I go to a case, the first thing I have to consider is whether or not I need a vet. The next question is, will the vet give me a ticket to have the horse put down? I have to consider if the case merits prosecution and if I do, I have to call a vet. I then have to ask the vets if they are prepared to go to court to prosecute and many are increasingly reluctant. But if I have a vet who says he will support prosecution, I then have to call the RSPCA, because they are the only people who can prosecute. They come along and we then have to call the police because they are the only ones who can seize horses and remove them to a place of safety. The police sign the horse over to us and then we have to find transport. But now when I call Claire and ask if I can bring another horse to the farm, the answer is sometimes 'no' because the farm is full. Throughout this whole procedure a horse might be in great distress.'

On one occasion, Phil found a horse stuck in a river. It was exhausted and struggling to keep its head above water. The quickest way to get it out was to call the fire brigade, who were soon on the scene. They immediately put up a safety perimeter to keep everyone back, including Phil, who wanted to hold the horse's head above the water. The fire team said it was against health and safety regulations – they had no choice, and the horse had to struggle alone in the water until eventually it was pulled out. The whole safety process had taken so long, though, that the horse eventually had to be put down. No one blames the firemen but sometimes you feel the object of the exercise – saving a horse from a swollen river or rescuing a pony from a patently dangerous or at least uncaring home on a housing estate – is often overlooked while the box ticking continues.

The reality is that horses and ponies are suffering today in the UK and something needs to be done to fast track justice for these blameless creatures. The main charities have got to work together because no one charity can do it alone. When there is a big case, one of the charities, such as WHW or Redwings, may act as a co-ordinator for the rescue but each of the other charities will take in a number of the horses. This strikes me as too little and, for many, too late. The wheels of justice must start turning faster because at the moment all I see in the developed world are problems and no solutions.

How do you stop a kindly old lady 'rescuing' yet another pony from a sale and then turning it out into a field with a dozen or more other ponies? At the sales they are only too happy to be rid of another unwanted pony but, as we have so often seen, what happens when that well-meaning lady can no longer cope, or loses the field she has been renting from a local farmer? She cannot afford to pay hundreds of pounds a month in livery so she turns to the local rescue centre. Should she be prevented from buying the pony in the first place? Who has the right to stop her and, even if they did, who would police the sales and check the financial affairs of those bidding? At some sales it is a case of 'Buy one, get one free', like some supermarket special offer. Far from wanting to put up barriers to prevent unsuitable purchasers, the auctioneers and owners are desperate to get rid of unwanted stock.

Even if all agree that there are too many horses and ponies and that the only answer is to put down the unwanted ones who have no possible quality of life ahead of them, it is not that easy, as the field officers at Glenda Spooner Farm point out. The brutal fact is that there are very few 'knackermen' left. In fact, there are only five slaughterhouses in this country licensed to dispose of horses for dog meat and of those, only three are operating. Towards the end of 2014 there was a six-week waiting list to get into one of those and there is no other outlet apart from hunt kennels. Even these are struggling to meet the stringent and expensive new rules regarding the safe disposal of horses. There was a time when the hair would have been used for stuffing furniture but that market has long gone. All this means it is much easier from a financial point of view to abandon horses than to have them humanely destroyed.

HALL FARM, NORFOLK

Hall Farm, Snetterton is the headquarters of WHW and the central hub which takes calls from all over the country to alert field officers of cases which need attention. I always say that the charity's front line is made up of the operators manning the hotline switchboard, which receives some 6,000 welfare calls a year. They have to decide whether the call is genuine or malicious and whether a field officer has to go out and investigate. Sometimes the calls are well intentioned but misplaced. Someone might say a Shetland pony does not have a rug on in the rain, when its own woolly coat with its natural insulation is proof enough against the harshest weather. Other calls are more serious and some are borderline.

The switchboard, manned by people with extensive equine knowledge, might get a call from someone who says that a field officer needs to go out to look at a horse because it is a disgrace, swearing down the phone and insisting that someone needs to be there in the next two minutes. If the call is to a case in Scotland, though, it might take a field officer two days to get there. They are expecting someone to be on site instantly and if they can't be, we're 'useless'.

Or there will be someone who has been left a card by one of the field officers with the central number. They will also be swearing down the phone, asking what we are doing, coming into the field checking on their horses, and warning that the next time someone comes they will have a shotgun ready.

And then, in the middle of it all, there will be genuinely concerned people in tears, heartbroken at the sight of a horse or pony possibly neglected or injured. We are often told that it is our responsibility to go out and care for a horse in distress. We will always do what we can, but actually it is the owner's responsibility and welfare charities should be the last resort.

Like the other WHW centres, Hall Farm is fully equipped to rescue, treat and rehome the horses and ponies which need help every day; it can handle between 120 and 150 but its walls have to be flexible, sometimes taking in rescues from other parts of the country when their stables and fields are full. It has 540 acres, uses 250 for the centre and rents the remaining land out to a farmer who produces all the straw and hay that the centre needs.

Some people wonder why we don't have more, smaller farms but that proved to be an inefficient way of operating because it was not possible to get the economies of scale. WHW has calculated that most welfare cases in the UK can be reached within a radius of 50–100 miles of its four centres.

While Sue Hodgkins, the centre manager, and her team cope with the latest influx, the back office, in a different part of the complex, is working out how best to stretch the WHW resources both in the UK and internationally, while every week there seems to be a new request from the media asking for comment on another equine crisis – doping, horse meat for human consumption, the rights and wrongs of racing, 'dangerous' jumps or hunting. Indeed it has been one of Roly Ower's great achievements as Chief Executive to raise the charity's profile such that it has become the first port of call for definitive, evidence-based comment on horse welfare matters.

It costs £700,000 a year to run the whole operation at Snetterton, including every aspect of horse welfare, running the campaigns to highlight the desperate work which needs to be done and running the back office, which not only keeps the Hall Farm field officers on the road but also co-ordinates with the other three centres.

As so much depends on education, as every field officer will agree, there is a fully- equipped conference centre at Hall Farm with videos to explain the work that is being done and an opportunity to see first-hand the rehabilitation treatments which the grooms, vets and physios give to the horses. All the farms welcome visitors and they can always find a job for volunteers to do, even if it just means walking a pony on a leading rein, part of the process of teaching it to trust a human. For many people that may be a unique experience.

Sometimes it may seem like an uphill task for Roly Owers and his colleagues as they try to push the horse welfare case up the agenda. They need to fight their corner with politicians in Westminster and Brussels, trying to persuade them not only to pass better laws regarding transportation of animals, for instance, but also urging new measures to enforce those laws. As ever, these things are a matter of priority; governments and councils have plenty of people lobbying to push through their own particular agenda and resources are always tight. What does it matter if a few horses are suffering on a long cross-European journey when people are going hungry or whole economies are struggling to balance their books? It matters to the team in Snetterton and all the other WHW centres, because if we become a nation that does not care about animal welfare, then what else will we choose to neglect? A society's treatment of all living things, both animal and human, is a reflection on itself.

14 | HORSES AND US TOMORROW

Those of us who keep horses, ponies, donkeys or mules do so either because they provide us with pleasure and entertainment or – and these are by far the majority – because they are essential, possibly even for survival. But I wonder where in this chain we pause to think about life from the horse's point of view? It strikes me that whether we are hoping to breed the next Derby winner or trying to keep a bag of bones toiling for another year in the African sun, the order of priority is always man first, beast second. On the one hand it is for our prestige, fortune or satisfaction, while on the other it is the more worthy struggle to provide food for the family to eat.

When Ada Cole came across the desperate sight of neglected horses on the dockside in Antwerp waiting to be transported to the slaughterhouses of Europe, she was determined to speak up for them and, by extension, for every other equine which exists entirely for the benefit of mankind. My fear is that that strong voice is growing weaker, drowned out by the clamour of ever-growing demands put upon our animals. As in every walk of life, we seem to want more of everything and, just as in life, sometimes we can have too much; in the western developed countries we are accustomed to the throw-away society and we now treat our animals in the same cavalier manner. When we are bored with them, grow out of them or they become too decrepit, we simply discard them as we might do an outdated mobile phone.

At the WHW 2014 Conference the theme was, 'What is the value of horses?' The answer to that is they have many and varied uses, from the seven million or more horses which died during World War One to the rehabilitation benefits described by Lance Corporal Jason Hare RM. He had suffered extensive injuries in Afghanistan but now, as a team leader for HorseBack UK, he was teaching others how learning to ride 'Western style' had helped him and many others to recover. It was 'cool to be a cowboy', he laughed, in the face of extreme adversity.

Roly Owers said: 'We should not assume that the different values that each of us imposes need to be in conflict. Each of us has our own perspective on horses which need not negate that of others.' But there is work to be done. 'Horses are sentient beings, they can feel fear, pain and distress... horse owners should treat their horses with respect because it is morally right and it is the law. Charities should not be used to clear up the mess left by people who systematically play the system,' he said. Above all, owners should remember to allow horses to be horses, neither over-pampered and kept in stables twenty-four hours a day, nor neglected or abandoned.

As things stand, the future for horses strikes me as full of danger; danger from neglect, from abuse, from ignorance and, so often, from greed. We must begin to question how we treat our horses and what we expect of them, and we must demand tougher action against those who wilfully mistreat these creatures.

I am the first to champion horse racing, but when does sport get overtaken by the relentless pursuit of winning at all and any cost? In the pursuit of 'more', we have more race meetings in the UK than we need; the fields are getting smaller, the quality of the racing is deteriorating, while all the time the pressure increases on the trainers to produce a winner to satisfy the owners who are paying the bills. The reality is that many two-year-olds actually start training as yearlings. They come into a trainer's yard as two-year-olds but they will not have been born on 1 January and that, of course, is one of the reasons why breeders try and get them to foal early, so they can run in April or May of the following year. I suppose the argument is you are competing like with like, but would those horses be better, stronger and even faster if they were left to mature? There is some evidence to show that a young horse's tendons might actually strengthen with some short races of a few furlongs over forgiving hurdles and on easy ground. There is inevitably an awful wastage because so many of the younger horses get injured, depending on how much work they are being made to do; possibly thousands fail to make the grade. I would like to think that most National Hunt trainers would ensure their horses are properly ridden, but how many of the lads and lasses have the ability to work, say, on the balance of a horse? If trainers have unlimited resources at their disposal, they can pick and choose the best riders. Equally they can pick and choose the best horses to race so the owners have the pleasure of seeing their colours in the winners' enclosure. But for smaller yards, with only a handful of horses and where the pockets are not quite so deep, the cheapest available labour is used, and the temptation is to run whenever possible to pick up all too elusive victories. Yards push on to try to get a winner when, in their heart of hearts, trainers know the ground may be too firm, but they decide that the risk to the horse's legs is worth taking.

Shrinking prize money in the less prestigious meetings following the over-expansion of racing will inevitably mean that some smaller trainers will go to the wall, with consequent misery for their families, staff and suppliers. Let me speak here, though, for the horses which will then become surplus to requirements. They may have been bought or bred in a moment of passion, but the risks in the racing game are huge and there are many more losers than winners. What to do with an unwanted racehorse with perhaps few, if any, wins to its name? There is only one answer.

The horse racing industry cannot look to the bookmakers to come to the rescue. Quite the reverse, in fact. Ladbrokes' Chief Executive Richard Glynn reports a serious decline in horse-race betting. 'If turnover trends do not improve and if the current cost structures are maintained for horse betting in particular, it may rapidly reach the point where it becomes unsustainable as a product,' he said (*Sunday Telegraph*, 24 August 2014).

An even sadder prospect is that there may not even be a new generation interested in watching racing regularly, with too many other distractions competing for their attention. As Tom Kerr warned: '...racing must find its fans of tomorrow. Fail to do so and a sad future lies ahead, with tracks as glorified beer gardens and the thoroughbred cast in the ignominious role of equine roulette ball.' (*Racing Post*, 17 August 2014). What a depressing thought. Perhaps the decline of the racing industry is not a strictly horse welfare problem, but it will have an impact. The current strategy is unsustainable. Racing should not be completely controlled by the bookmakers. It does not require more and more racing to generate levy, but a reduction in the quantity and an improvement in the quality. People are noticing and already voting with their feet. At the 2014 August meeting at York, the attendance at Ladies' Day, which normally attracts a good crowd, was noticeably down, by around 12,000 on the previous year.

York, which is just one example, used to have three highly successful midweek days which were about the best three days racing you could hope for, but what have they done? They have extended it by a day, starting a day later so they now run into Saturday. In the round they will make a bit more money, but it is probably to the detriment of the sport because there may not be enough top-class horses to fill more races. I understand that the accountants have to watch the figures and the course has to go on updating its facilities, but in many cases this just means more and more corporate hospitality boxes. Boxes are expensive and not every racegoer wants to use them, preferring instead to mill about among the crowds. Looking at the next generation of future punters and racing fans, I am convinced the present system is becoming unbalanced and in danger of becoming too expensive.

Still worse, there is potential danger in excessive, poor quality racing as the *Racing Post* columnist, Alastair Down, wrote: '...as we greedily encourage more and more dreadful racing we inevitably encourage yet more horses hailing from yards with ever more inadequate facilities. More racing equals the potential for more disaster.' (*The Best of Alastair Down*, Racing Post Books).

It may be a forlorn hope but I also bemoan the disappearance of amateurism in the last vestiges of supposedly non-professional race riding, point-to-pointing. This definitely has a bearing on horse welfare because it relates to pursuing the prize at all costs and failing to enjoy the sport for its own pleasure. The amateur aspect is declining because there are trainers running sizeable stables of horses with staff who work full time. They are using the top jockeys, some of whom are ostensibly amateurs but who, without doubt, are paid per ride, and that is absolutely against the ethos of the sport.

In fact the ethos of the true amateur has all but vanished, as it has already done in many other sports too, such as rowing, rugby and golf. I do not begrudge that but where are the real amateurs who have to hold down a city job at the same time? My son, Philip, is one. As an amateur rider, unless you are extremely lucky, you do not get to ride one of the top jumpers, for example, because they are in the hands of the leading ten stables. They will have full-time grooms and, if they are good enough, they would hope to get rides. To get going as a true amateur, coming up through the Pony Club, your parents have to buy the horses until, if you are lucky enough, you land a sponsor or chance your luck with a horse out of a licensed trainer's yard that has been unable to win good National Hunt races or has proved too old to do so. As I say, to see a return to amateurism is a forlorn hope from someone who has enjoyed competing and knowing that there was always a chance of winning because most of those other 'jockeys', like me, would have to return to their desks on the following Monday morning.

On the other hand it could be argued that life has moved on: as standards have improved across the board, so have the top performers at all levels. Fifty years ago a farmer, the equivalent of today's 'pro', may have been given a few bottles as a prize or fee. But point-to-pointing is undoubtedly declining and that is as much to do with the prohibitive cost of keeping a horse in training, and possibly even urban spread, as with gentleman farmers who want to keep competing, leaving just the true professionals in a much depleted field.

The issue of drug abuse in equine sports has been covered and I would assume that all agree it should be outlawed, but two questions remain: consistency over what is illegal and what is not, and whether the punishment always fits the crime. If a drug is used to enhance performance, there is no place for it in equestrian or indeed any other sport and that should surely be consistent throughout the world. Secondly, when abusers are detected, they should be thrown out of the game altogether with no chance of reprieve, because once they have been tempted to break the law, they will be tempted again. Furthermore, they can never be trusted and their abuse will never be forgotten – the all-seeing internet will ensure that their record will follow them. Sadly, as we have discussed, in the case of equestrian sports, a horse which has won a race as a result of steroids will always have the 'benefit' of those drugs in its system – stronger muscles, improved stamina – and the cloud of suspicion will hang over any future result, so they, too, should be stopped from racing again.

Laws are in place for the protection of all and in this case my first concern is for the horses. They have no choice in the matter but, while their instinct may be to run fast, they need to be protected from running faster than their bodies are naturally capable of doing. How can it be acceptable for a racehorse to run until its lungs bleed? What is happening to the sport so many of us enjoyed? Who is going to save it from itself?

There are risks involved in all equestrian sports; with the exception of dressage and showing classes, they are more often than not undertaken at speed, there are sometimes obstacles to be tackled, even very big obstacles in the world of eventing, for example. Technology, though, is on our side with frangible pins and foam logs, and no three-day event rider likes to see a fall. Tragically there are still some fatalities and we have to acknowledge concerns. 'The cross country course design has become too challenging,' says Dene Stanstall of Animal Aid. 'They risk breaking the horses' necks or backs.' (*Time* magazine, 28 July 2012). The riders themselves are very well aware of those risks and constantly seek new ways to protect both their horses and themselves while ensuring that nothing is lost from the thrill and the spectacle of cross-country riding. Francis Whittington, 2014 UK National Event Riding Champion, winner of Blenheim International Horse Trials and former chairman of the Event Riders' Association, puts the counter argument: 'Riders are aware of the risks they take and they know what their horses are capable of doing. Even in the middle of a cross-country course, if I have felt that my horse was not going well I would pull up rather than take a chance. Riders are so attuned to the moods, strengths and weaknesses of their horses that they can literally feel when something is wrong. One thing is certain, no rider would put his horse at an obstacle that it was not capable of jumping. There is a tremendous trust between horse and rider and the hours of training and schooling to prepare for three day eventing ensures that the sport is as safe as possible. The last point I would make is that the cross-country course designers, such as Mark Phillips, are often former top event riders who know what can and cannot be done. Their aim is always to prepare a challenging but safe course – the last thing they want to see is a tremendous number of fallers. A ducking in the Badminton Lake is one thing which amuses the crowd, but usually it is the rider not the horse that looks a bit of a fool.'

Are we sometimes just asking too much of our horses? Are the jumps too challenging? I am prepared to let the riders be the judge of that because the very great majority of them care so much about their horses. In the 2014 World Equestrian Games, Wild Lone, a 13-year-old ridden by Britain's Harry Meade, collapsed and died after riding a clear round in the cross-country phase. The going had been heavy at Haras du Pin in Normandy and some fences had been taken out of the course, but had it all been too much for the horse? Harry Meade was adamant that the going had no bearing on what happened. Speaking shortly afterwards: 'The ground's conditions and terrain I felt played no part whatsoever in what happened to Wild Lone. This is his sixth four-star event, he hadn't missed any work, he was as fit as any horse I have had as a four star and he gave me a wonderful ride.'

Accidents do happen and sometimes there can be tragic consequences. In one terrible week in October 2014 three racing jockeys – Carly-Mae Pye, Caitlin Forrest and apprentice Juan Saez – all died as a result of falls in Australia and America, but the sport is leading the way in safety features to minimise the risks wherever possible. As racing correspondent, Marcus Armytage, put it in his column: 'Injury, paralysis or worse are an occupational hazard of working with horses, animals that weigh half a tonne, have minds of their own and, usually, four metal-plated feet.' (*Daily Telegraph*, 18 October 2014).

The vast majority of horse, donkey and mule owners, of course, will never read this book because their lives are entirely consumed with eking out a living rather than relaxing at the races. We can all, though, help them look after their beasts of burden in a better way. Equines make the developing world function and eventually, if that world can prosper, we will all benefit. I know that giving money to help educate a farmer in Africa about how to care for his mule's hooves is a tougher charitable sell than asking people to give to Oxfam, Cancer Research or a children's hospice, but it is remarkable how very little can have a very great impact. When WHW teams arrive in a village and train one man how to make shoes for a horse or create a better fitting harness for it to pull a heavily-laden cart, it does not take long for the message to spread, for him to be able to train others and for a greater, sustainable income stream to be formed.

There is still a failure of communication between the valuable work of human development organisations and animal charities operating around the world. All those attending the WHW-sponsored 2014 Colloquium on Working Equids agreed that there was a need to find ways of improving understanding of each others' work because, so often, these agencies will find themselves working in similar situations – helping the victims of earthquakes and floods, getting vital supplies to the needy, teaching communities a better way of farming and improving their standard of living.

The Colloquium attendees agreed: 'It is incumbent on us to provide good quality information to allow communication and improve awareness, and this information is needed to underpin the one-health one-welfare approach. We need to make it clear what we can offer, and be honest about what we can't do; to look for points of convergence and common areas of interest and need to be able to promote a long term holistic approach. One analogy for a preventive approach was that we should consider, 'instead of being an ambulance at the bottom of the cliff, be the fence at the top.'

Are we at WHW, along with our fellow charities SPANA, The Brooke and The Donkey Sanctuary, making a difference in developing countries? I believe the answer is an emphatic yes because one better-shod horse or donkey is a healthier animal that will live longer and serve its owner for years to come.

While there will always be important work to be done in the UK, WHW anticipates that the international side will increase, doubling the number of countries in which it operates in the next three years, and Barry Johnson, chairman, believes this can only be done effectively by working alongside other charities. 'The danger,' he said, 'is that we go into countries and work in silos – animal aid and human aid groups do valuable but independent work which does not reach the wider community. Those sorts of links are important. So we are moving away from just teaching people farriery and saddlery and advising on nutrition involving the whole community, teaching children in schools about hygiene and about transmitting disease between horses and between horses and humans. I think this is the way forward because basic hygiene about cleaning out water buckets also applies in the homes. Just treating the horse will always only be 'just treating the horse' and our aim is not just to treat the horse but help the family, and if another charity is working with the family we can achieve so much more than just by working alone.'

At home in the UK, among the 180,000 charities trying to attract the public's attention and its money, there are some 150 equine charities, which is possibly too many. The majority of these are very local, small sanctuaries, others will be operating on a charitable basis but not registered as such and then, of course, there are many other multi-species charities such as the RSPCA that include equines in their charitable objectives. There are 15 equine charities in the UK with an income of more than £1 million. The Donkey Sanctuary is the largest 'equine' charity in the country, followed by The Brooke and a number in and around the £7–£10 million bracket (including BHS, Redwings and World Horse Welfare).

As WHW campaigns highlight, people must first ask themselves whether they really do need a horse or a pony. If the answer is yes then, crucially, they must be fully aware of the implications and obligations. One of the other dangers is that the hobby turns into an obsession and before very long a herd of semi-feral ponies has developed. We need to remember, though, that it is not just the professionals who breed: adding one more foal 'to continue the bloodline' potentially adds to the problem. WHW predicts – as do, no doubt, all the other equine charities that pick up the pieces when owners can no longer cope - that the problem of over-breeding is getting worse. If animal sanctuaries and rehoming stables are already full to capacity with almost every size and shape of horse, why run the risk of breeding another animal which may develop a problem? People should remember that WHW offers a 'lifetime guarantee' to monitor the health of the horses and ponies they rehome and will always take them back when and if the rehomers can no longer cope, for one reason or another. It is probably a unique proposition.

WHW is committed to investing more time, effort and money in education and awareness at home in the UK. It knows it could spend its entire budget on domestic operations and still only reach a fraction of the horses and ponies in urgent need of care in Britain alone. What is remarkable is that so many who regard themselves as part of the horse world have no concept of the underworld that exists in the sport or the dark underbelly of sales markets, and simply just drive on past. Laws are important but they cannot achieve very much in themselves without adequate enforcement. There needs to be collective responsibility, because the care of horses starts with horse owners; there is a tendency to blame everyone else except themselves, they fail to notice what goes on in livery yards, even sometimes mistaking over-zealous care for kindness when it may, in fact, amount to cruelty. It may be necessary to challenge the status quo on how we look after our horses, even at the highest levels of equestrian competition. Keeping a horse in its stable twenty four hours a day, seven days a week is wrong, no matter how much we think we love them or how precious we think they are.

There is no one-size-fits-all solution to the question of how we protect horses. There are so many differences. There are differences among the equestrian sports – show jumpers and event riders differ and so do jockeys in horse racing. There is a difference in the style of riding – controlled aggression of racing versus the subtle sensitivity of dressage, the stamina of event riding versus the explosive power of show jumping. A three-mile steeple chase requires different breeding and quite a different technique to a five-furlong sprint. 'Horses for courses', one might say, and the riding is completely different. Throw into that mix the variety of riding styles from country to country and even the cultural differences between nations; the British approach is almost a bond between rider and horse. Among some other nations, I don't detect that same closeness; the horses will always be animals, never anything approaching a pet. Having made such sweeping generalisations, I acknowledge that there have been and will always be bad apples in every discipline, pushing and abusing their horses to respond to the rider's commands. What has riding come to when endurance riding has been forced to introduce tough rules to clean up the sport which was plagued during 2014 with cheating, doping and even fatalities? Fixed and mobile surveillance cameras more suited to the world of espionage than racecourses have even been introduced at some events to catch the ringers and the dopers. John McEwen, FEI Vice President, warned the national federations that '...the eyes of the world are upon us,' to see if the sport could clean up its act.

Meanwhile, 80% of the world's equines remain at hard, honest and painful work, and I wonder what we can do to help them. Sometimes all it takes is a place for them to pause, shelter from the sun and have a drink of water. It is not high technology, it is simple humanity. If only someone were available to explain some basic points of farriery and harness making so that the hooves would not ache and the shafts of the cart would not rub the donkey's sides raw. Or think laterally, as we do in Honduras, and work with the forestry authorities to plant fast-growing trees nearer towns and villages. This not only protects forests but saves horses and ponies, making daily treks, sometimes of ten kilometres, to haul firewood back to communities so that they can do their cooking.

It is plain to me that the law, with which I started this book, is unable to make a difference. The law cannot reach the villages of Africa; it cannot even make a difference in Europe, where transporters haul live horses thousands of miles for slaughter.

The solution, as so often with crime, is to begin with education. By educating horse owners about the rudiments of caring for hooves, by educating owners about the basic dangers of laminitis, by educating children about the responsibilities of owning a horse, then at least we will be making a difference.

By collaborating with universities in the UK and overseas we can help students with their course work and give practical experience to veterinary students in the field. Everyone benefits: the students learn and can share their experiences with their colleagues back in the classroom, and animals benefit from the treatment they receive. There is a danger, as WHW President, the Princess Royal, ever practical, has often pointed out, that we get so tied up with the science and diagnostics that we forget about the horse. She asks: how are you going to make the horses better? And of course she is right, because while science may have advanced, specific new treatments have only moved a few steps forward.

The horse has been integral to our world since prehistoric times as the cave paintings in Chauvet, in southern France, beautifully illustrate. It has been domesticated for some five and a half thousand years, which means we have been reliant upon it for all that time to hunt, to fight and to work, and yet we are still mistreating it. What would human civilisation have been without the horse? Over the centuries we have admired it, raced it, even worshipped it, and without it the mighty warriors of the past – Alexander the Great or even Genghis Khan would have achieved little; the Romans would not have extended their empire, the development of America might have been different had the Spanish Conquistadors not introduced horses to the Plains Indians, essentially a pedestrian people, and perhaps even our landscape would have been different without horses to plough the fields. There is so much to admire and to be grateful for, there is absolutely nothing to decry, and that is why we must all speak up for the horse.

We have to keep the voice of Ada Cole alive and ringing in people's ears. Remember what she said: 'It is because people do not want to hear that nothing is done. I am going to make people listen.' And she told us that it is our duty to hear.

A brief history of World Horse Welfare

1927 – Ada Cole founds the International League for the Protection of Horses (ILPH) after seeing work-worn horses on the docks of Antwerp, destined for slaughter.

1937 – The ILPH-driven Exportation of Horses Act is introduced, effectively stopping the export of live horses for slaughter from Great Britain.

1949 – ILPH's first rehabilitation centre opens in Britain.

1952–1954 – Introduction of Acts protecting horses transported by sea and at slaughterhouses, thanks in large part to the ILPH.

1950–1965 – ILPH engages in activities to improve horse welfare in France, Italy, the Netherlands, Germany, Spain, Greece and South Africa.

1978 – ILPH rehomes scores of old police horses and pit ponies, emerging as the largest equine rehoming charity in Britain.

1985 – ILPH's first international training course is launched in Morocco after encouragement from Sir Peter O'Sullevan.

1994 – ILPH hands a petition bearing 3,286,645 signatures to the European Parliament to demonstrate public feeling against long-distance journeys of horses to slaughter.

HRH The Princess Royal becomes ILPH President.

2007 – Regulation (EC) No 1/2005 comes into force, improving conditions for horses transported long distance to slaughter in Europe. While incorporating some of ILPH's recommendations, this legislation still does not go far enough.

2008 – ILPH is re-branded as World Horse Welfare.

The charity becomes associate member of the International Equestrian Federation (FEI) after almost three decades as their welfare advisors.

2010 – Written declaration highlighting the horrific slaughter transport trade is adopted by the European Parliament.

Today – World Horse Welfare is a leading international charity that improves the lives of horses in the UK and worldwide through education, campaigning and hands-on care. Working across four continents, its whole approach is practical, based on scientific evidence and extensive experience, and focused on delivering lasting change across the full spectrum of the horse world. As Britain's largest horse rescue and rehoming charity, World Horse Welfare runs four Rescue and Rehoming Centres and works tirelessly to change legislation and attitudes to horse welfare through campaigns and education across Europe. Its international programmes alleviate the suffering of working horses by providing essential knowledge for horse-owning communities in the developing world, and its work with sport regulators helps to maintain and improve welfare standards in racing and equestrian sport.

Index